On Literature and Aesthetics

Aesthetics

Nigel Pearce

Published by
Chipmunkapublishing
United Kingdom

http://www.chipmunkapublishing.com

Marxist Literary Aesthetics or continuities and discontinuities in three novels: Ivan Turgenev's Fathers and Sons, Victor Serge's Conquered City and China Miéville's The City and The City?

Abstract.

This dissertation is orientated to possibly the most pivotal moment of modernity. Its repercussions and echoes are still heard in both the ears of class-conscious proletarians who are inspired to write and aspire towards elevated aesthetic endeavour and the bourgeoisie that shakes in their handmade boots at its very mention. This event was the October revolution in Russia of 1917. However, it was a revolution betrayed by the nefarious Stalinist bureaucracy. Marxist literary theory has a dialectical and interactive relationship between the base and superstructure. Hence there is intercourse between the socio-economic and cultural. However, as literature is intertextual so are aesthetics. Thus, my argument is made in the context of Western aesthetics and will find the solution to Kant's 'subject-object' problem not in his individualist synthetic a priori but in a Lukacsian 'identical-subject-object' of the proletariat where the full creative power of humanity will be released. To paraphrase Trotsky every woman and man will rise to the heights of an Aristotle, a Goethe, a Marx, a Christina Rossetti, or a Sappho. Turgenev's Fathers and Sons will be seen to foreshadow the revolution, Victor Serge's novel Conquered City will be understood as a product of its contradictory beliefs and times quoting Serge 'defeat-in-victory.' Finally, China Melville's Weird Fiction in general and even when combined with a detective genre in The City and The City can be comprehended as a literary response to the revolution's defeat in terms of genre. My argument follows both Lukacs and Terry Eagleton, The Real Thing Reflections on a Literary Form (London, Yale University Press, 2024) in arguing for variations on the genre of 'critical realism' as the way ahead for proletarian fiction. I look to the late John Molyneux's innovatory contribution to

Marxist aesthetics The Dialectic of Art (Chicago, Haymarket, 2020) as a source for potential further research into this field. A note on style. On occasion my writing can adopt a dialectical nature. I am interested, particularly, in the application of the Marxist aesthetic, Historical and Dialectical Materialism, to my primary texts.

Personal Statement.

Although my methodology is consistently Marxist or Marxist-feminist throughout my academic work. I have not addressed these novels previously or in this precise manner.

Contents Page.

Chapters.

Chapter One introduction: Aesthetics and the Marxist Literary Aesthetic. An unbroken thread?

Chapter Two: Ivan Turgenev as a Realist novelist and Bazanov as a failed revolutionary in Fathers and Sons? Or a bifurcation between Turgenev's concepts of Hamlet and Don Quixote?

Chapter Three. Victor Serge Conquered City: a tale of contradictory beliefs and times.

Chapter Four. China Melville's The City and The City: the defeat of a revolution and the death of a genre.

Conclusion. Nineteenth and Twentieth century Russia: a laboratory for literature. Results and Prospects or continuities and discontinuities?

Chapter One: Introduction: Aesthetics and the Marxist
Literary Aesthetic. An unbroken thread?
The intention in this introduction is to provide a theoretical
and methodological structure for the analysis of the three
primary texts. I will argue that following the young Marx
'Communism is the riddle of history solved and it knows itself
to be the solution.' Followed by sections illustrating the
arguments of Aristotle, while recognizing the immense
significance of the Renaissance and Enlightenment on
humanist thought through Kant, and Hegel to the Marxist
literary aesthetic. I will conclude that after the failure of
Classical German philosophy and aesthetics to solve the
'subject-object' problem this was corrected by Lukács in his
formulation of the proletarian 'identical-subject-object,' the
working class as the totality in communism. Also, I suggest
that the methodology of Historical Materialism and
Dialectical Materialism has an inherent propensity toward
Realism as a genre and illustrate this in both the writings of
Marx, and particularly, two late letters from Engels. In
conclusion I shall suggest that the Marxist tradition following
Adolfo Sanchez Vazquez finds its fruition in 'a society of
men-artists.' Also, this analysis will find the recent aesthetic
outlined by John Molyneux Dialectics of Art to be innovative.
Thus, I continue with an exploration of Aristotle's Poetics. In
Poetics, Aristotle sketched what would become the dominant
form of Western aesthetics; indeed, its contents remain
pertinent. The primary twentieth century's only serious
development as a method of literary aesthetics is Bertolt
Brecht's theory of the 'alienation effect', which challenges
later versions of Aristotle's theory such as Freytag's Triangle
because it disrupts the causal nature of literary art as
suggested by Aristotle. In modernity or even postmodernity,
which Frederick Jameson argued is 'the logic of late
capitalism,' these models have not entirely disintegrated into
montage. For Aristotle, there were several forms of art, the
highest of which was tragedy, and is presumed by many that
he believed Sophocles was its greatest exponent. However,
this passage complicates this apparent conventional
knowledge of the origins of Aristotle's aesthetics:

chapter 17 [of Poetics] is in fact based on Euripides' Iphigeneia in Tauris, which he cites as often as Sophocles' Oedipus, although the two plays are very different. It is a fundamental mistake to suppose that Aristotle's theory of tragedy as a whole is modelled exclusively on the Oedipus, or applicable primarily to plays of that kind. .

Aristotle created two fundamental pillars on which he built his aesthetic in Poetics: a) mimesis or imitation of the world as a representation and b) the ordering of the artistic act. In, tragedy which Aristotle believed is the highest form of literature, the audience should experience a catharsis at the conclusion. This was and is a social mechanism whereby social tensions are acted out, creating an emotional response in the audience which are and then purged at the conclusion. However, as Augusto Boal explains, it was, essentially, an artistic means of social control.   So, social tensions are transmogrified into dramatic ones.

For Kant made an immense shift from aesthetics with a 'purpose' emanating from both Plato and Aristotle to one of 'purposeless purposefulness.' I shall address Emmanuel Kant's ideas about the voice of the author's individuality and the concept of 'genius,' which I will contest in that it will be understood as a product of the rise of the bourgeois individual and the early development of capitalism. Thus, I shall consistently apply my methodology. In this area, the great Hungarian thinker Georg Lukács wanted to understand why bourgeois philosophy –, principally Classical German Philosophy, typified by Immanuel Kant and Hegel – had not solved the central problem of philosophy of their epoch: that is, of, the relationship of the subject to the object, a problem of epistemology rather than that of the question of aesthetics alone. This had previously manifested itself to Kant in the two schools of thought.

Firstly, there were the: Rationalists who believed thought was paramount and was a preliminary to the knowledge of the world if it was possible to know it. Thus, thought was a priori or before anterior to human experience. Manifestations of this school would be pure mathematics and ontological proofs of the existence of God.

Alternatively, the empiricists of a British school of philosophers, especially Locke and Hume, believed human knowledge was a posteriori or after experience. Humans are tabula rasa, they believed, a blank slate on which experience makes its marks. This is associated with justification that depends on experience or empirical evidence, as with most aspects of science.

Kant Critique of Judgement made an original series of possible aesthetic judgements and was published in 1790 . He recognised he was developing his ideas in a new yet not unconnected direction to his previous Critiques. The first part of Critique of Judgement sketches four areas of aesthetic reflective judgments which are of a different nature to his determinate judgements of the previous critiques. The first part of Kant's Critique of Aesthetic Judgement presents what Kant calls the four moments of the "Judgement of Taste". These are given by Kant in sequence as the (1) First Moment. Of the Judgement of Taste: Moment of Quality"; (2) Second Moment. Of the Judgement of Taste: Moment of Quantity"; (3) Third Moment: Of Judgement of Taste: Moment of the Relation of the ends brought under Review in such Judgements"; and (4) Fourth Moment: Of the Judgement of Taste: Moment of the Modality of the Delight in the Object". After the presentation of the four moments of the Judgement of Taste, Kant then begins his discussion of Book 2 of the Third Critique titled Analytic of the Sublime. Firstly, the judgement of 'the agreeable' are sensory judgments like 'chocolate is nice,' a purely subjective judgment. 'The good' is rather an ethical judgment made in accordance with morals which for Kant are of an objective. This leaves 'the beautiful' and 'the sublime.' These are differentiated from subjective agreeable and objective good because Kant designates them 'subjective universal judgements.' The other two judgments — the beautiful and the sublime — thus differ from both the agreeable and the good. They are what Kant refers to as "subjective universal" judgments. This means that the judgments are subjective and are not tied to any absolute and determinate concept. However, the judgment that something is beautiful, or sublime is made with a supposition that others "ought" to share this judgment — even though it is known that many will not. The force of this "ought" is derived from a reference to a sensus communis — a community of taste. For Kant, the capacity of genius is that of being to recognise and produce the beautiful and sublime. I argue that this is determined by the socio- economic conditions in which Kant was writing i.e. the advent of capitalism and is a bourgeois individualist position. This will, I suggest, be qualitatively transformed by the proletariat into a universalised, totalised, and socialised aesthetic in which all women and men will be comrade artists.

Kant's concept of 'disinterestedness' had consequences for writers in the 19th and 20th centuries such as Matthew Arnold and T.S. Eliot. The latter who in his conservative literary criticism which is interestingly juxtaposed with his experimental early modernist poetry where he comments rather caustically in Tradition and Individual Talent:

Poetry is not a turning loose of emotion, but an escape from emotion; it is not the expression of personality, but an escape from personality. But, of course, only those who have personality and emotions know what it means to want to escape from these things.

Following A.E. Bradley Oxford Lectures on Poetry, Hegel's Theory of Tragedy. I argue that a qualitative transformation in aesthetics took place with Kant and Hegel as a response to the Renaissance and the Enlightenment. This can be persuasively understood as a movement away from tragedy to be seen in the realm of the gods in Ancient Greece e.g. the plays Oedipus and Antigone to the humanism of the Italian Renaissance typified in Petrarch and later in the plays of Shakespeare such as Romeo and Juliet and Schiller, The Wanderers, that address conflicts not between the gods but within a common humanity. This cannot be over emphasized as it transformed literary aesthetics and literature. Tragedy like the dialectic can only function with conflict because as Hegel argued 'contradiction lies at the heart of all things. Hegel delineates his position on the artist and writer thus:

Art's vocation, Hegel says, is to unveil the truth in the form of sensuous artistic configuration, to set forth the reconciled opposition [between the worlds of thought and sense] ... and so to have its end and aim in itself. For other ends, like instruction, purification, bettering, financial gain, struggling for fame and honour, have nothing to do with the work of art as such, and do not determine its nature.

Further and moreover, I suggest and as Sullivan and Gluckstein maintain, that '[t]to understand Hegel [...]it is important to be aware that Hegel was writing shortly after the death of Kant. . This is essential to my argument about the 'subject- object' problem, the inability of Classical German philosophy to solve it, and Lukács' remedy in the 'identical- subject-object' of the proletariat. Therefore, here I coalesce around the Kant-Hegel question to contrast it with the solutions provided by Marxist aesthetics. Thus, an understanding of Hegel is essential to this argument and can only be understood in the context of Kant. Hence, it is necessary to reexamine Kant, who was a theist, who after reading the sceptic, Hume. Kant was minded solving the subject-object problem. He argued that we can see a phenomenological world but cannot know because it is merely that of 'appearances.' However, beyond this lies the world of essences we cannot understand through the senses. This he called the noumenal world or 'things-in-themselves.' We cannot see that world like the phenomenological world, which consists of 'things-as-they-appear-to-us.' He tried to fuse the two with a synthetic a priori. Thus, we can learn about the world, 'matters of fact,' just by thinking. Had he persuasively solved the subject-object problem? No, argued Georg Lukács, because the two were not combined into a synthesis to form an 'identical subject-object.' Lukács maintained the possibility that this could only be solved dialectically and thus with knowledge of Hegelian philosophy and dialectics. Also, this would be solved in a Materialist manner because Marx had inverted Hegel and be manifest, ultimately, in Realist literature. Marx significantly 'turned Hegel on his head.' 8. In the last instance, I will argue, that we can perceive a literary current from Aristotle's verisimilitude to Lukács critical realism. If not an unbroken thread at least a series of echoes. Thus, only a Socialist society where class contradictions have been eliminated can create an innovative and proletarian aesthetic. Therefore, this introduction examines the methodology of aesthetics. For the Marxist critic György Lukács, whose views on realism we shall be considering later, realism is 'not a substitute for political action; it is the structure of consciousness that accompanies it.' .

Thus, I shall sketch out in more detail the Marxist philosophical and literary aesthetic and how the latter can be seen as a cogent methodology for the interpretation of the chosen novels. It is necessary to orientate my analysis in the context of aesthetics as I shall explore György Lukács intertwining of philosophy and literary criticism in the context of Trotsky's contributions. Two essential letters from Engels will introduce my concluding signposting to the novels of Turgenev, Serge, and Miéville, synthesising primary and secondary materials. I will also, examine Serge's, and Miéville's concepts about literary theory. Finally, I will explore Trotsky's and Adolfo Sanchez Vazquez's contributions to the debates on post-revolutionary literature. For the Marxist, the qualitatively different aspect of aesthetics is that it is de-alienated labour and because labour is humanity's 'species-being' This can be understood in Lukacsian terms as determined by 'the-identical -subject-object' of the working class under the conditions of communism, thus solving the problems posed by previous aesthetics. In the conclusion I shall illustrate a potential innovation in Marxist literary aesthetics in the Dialectics of Art published in 2020 written by John Molyneux which I find cogent.

The Marxist method has its most precise and fundamental delineation in a work by the young Marx, Preface to A Contribution to the Critique of Political Economy (1859):
In the social production of their life, men enter into definite relations that are indispensable and independent of their will, relations of production which correspond to a definite state of the development of their material productive forces. [...]. It

is not the consciousness of men that determines their being, but, on the contrary, their social being that determines their consciousness.

Herein lies the rational kernel of my method in that there is not only a material base for ideas and ideology but also a societal foundation. Men's and women's consciousness is moulded by the social environment in which they live. We see a leaning towards Realist literature in the method of Marxism. In a pertinent letter from Engels to Margret Harkness he provided a foundation for the Marxist Realist aesthetic:

If I have anything to criticize, it would be that perhaps, after all, the tale is not quite realistic enough. Realism, to my mind, implies, besides truth of detail, the truthful reproduction of typical characters under typical circumstances.

Now your characters are typical enough, as far as they go; but perhaps the circumstances which surround them and make them act, are not perhaps equally so. In the "City Girl" the working-class figures are a passive mass, unable to help. That Balzac thus was compelled to go against his own class sympathies and political prejudices, that he saw the necessity of the downfall of his favourite nobles, and described them as people deserving no better fate; and that he saw the real men of the future where, for the time being, they alone were to be found - that I consider one of the greatest triumphs of Realism, and one of the grandest features in old Balzac itself and not even showing (making) any attempt at striving to help itself

Here we can ascertain Engels delineating a later foundation of the theory of literary Marxist aesthetics. It was not a tendentious literature acting to persuade by 'telling.' Rather, its nature was that preferred by tutors in modern creative writing faculties, that of 'showing,' laying bear the inherent contradictions of the tale, of society.

Therefore, to debate Marxist aesthetics and their applications to three novels, Ivan Turgenev's Fathers and Sons, Victor Serge's Conquered City and China Miéville The

City and The City, I shall examine Marxist Literary Aesthetics in their historicised context. For as literature is intertextual, so are aesthetics. After delineating the literary aesthetic and its blooming into a complex and varied Marxist theory of literary aesthetics, I shall review the texts in that context. In Fathers and Sons, this will help us understand Turgenev's protagonist, Bazanov, as the ambiguous prototype of the literary 'the new man' Here was the male precursor to the 'new woman,' Vera Pavlovna, in Chernyshevsky's What is to be Done, see for example her first dream, Vera's "dream-guide" (a version of herself) introduces herself as "the bride of your [Vera's] bridegroom," solidifying Vera's intention to marry Lopukhov and free herself from her cellar. In her dream, Vera continues to free other young women from their own cellars. Vera does so in real life by forming her sewing co-operative and residential commune that affords both herself and other young women the ability to become financially independent and self-sufficient. The latter as Lenin's favourite novel. Lukács articulates an alternative view to the one I posit here at least: i.e. that, 'Turgenev—was an essentially Western European novelist of disillusionment—. Marx, in contradiction, argued about Turgenev: 'wonderfully renders the peculiarities of the Russian soul in its veiled Slavonic sensitivity'.

So, I suggest that after establishing two cultural precursors, the novels of Turgenev and Chernyshevsky as they both reflected the social and ideological contradictions in the conditions prior to the Russian Revolution. I will explore its defeat, as characterized by the decline by 1929, as Trotsky argues into a 'Degenerated Worker's State', or, later, as argued by Tony Cliff, a form of 'bureaucratic state capitalism'. . This defeat had ramifications for the debates on Marxist literary aesthetics and, indeed, the production of all literary texts in its wake. Thus, Victor Serge's Conquered City will be examined in the context of what the author designated as 'the midnight of the century' which was the title of his novel that encapsulated the Stalinist betrayal of the October revolution. In 1933, Victor Serge was arrested by Stalin's police, interrogated, and held in solitary confinement for more than eighty days. Then he spent two years in exile in remote Orenburg. These experiences were the inspiration for Midnight of the Century, Serge's novel about revolutionaries living in the shadow of Stalin's betrayal of the revolution. Therefore, I will also discuss the novel in the context of Serge's and Trotsky's debates on the nature of the USSR and its consequences for their literary perspectives. Serge differed from Trotsky's position because he believed 'the germ of Stalinism was in Bolshevism.' . Trotsky argued that a combination of external and internal forces was responsible. I shall return to Engels in a late letter to Mehring, in which there is the expression of a comprehensive theory of dialectical literary criticism. Then, I will recollect the polemic between Lukács and Ernst Bloch over subjectivity and

Expressionism in literature. I shall understand this as having implications in the last instance, for the text of China Miéville's The City and The City in the context of this literary journal revealed in the following interview:

The world is post-lapsarian; therefore, it is Tragic and a Vale of Sorrows. In other words, the fucked-up mess and intrinsic tensions have been explained away. It's tragic and sad, but it still consoles in that it smooth over everyday tensions. We got kicked out of the garden; the elves left—what do you expect?

I try to avoid it with various techniques. One is to undercut narrative security— I would claim that the endings of my books aren't downbeat, but they certainly try to undermine straightforward closure. There is closure, but it's often emotional or thematic rather than narrative.

The other thing, of course, is a continuing refusal to posit societies as internally coherent, consistent, bounded, and essentially safe. They are fractured and dangerous. The dynamics tearing them apart (the dynamics that lead to narrative) are intrinsic. .

Therefore, I would maintain that because of the dialectical contradictions which will create the class conflict which can only be resolved in a qualitatively different society for as Marx suggested and therefore Miéville could have misconstrued the nature of classical Marxism (see also my later comments on his deviation from unorthodox Trotskyism, for example):

The monopoly of capital becomes a fetter upon the mode of production, which has sprung up and flourished with and under it. The centralization of the means of production and the socialization of labour at last reach a point where they become incompatible with their capitalist integument. The integument is burst asunder. The knell of capitalist property sounds. The ex-proprietors are expropriated.

Thus, Marx argued that because the proletariat must or 'in the last instance' create a totality of an 'identical-subject-object' which is manifest in Communism, this is because, for Lukács, the proletariat has an 'ascribed consciousness.,' an idea he had derived from Weber's concept of ideal types.

Therefore, although the proletariat as a group of individuals may not seem the class whose 'world-historic mission' it is to create Communism, they will, as Marx and Engels argued in The German Ideology purge themselves 'of the muck of ages' in the process:

The revolution is necessary, therefore, not only because the ruling class cannot be overthrown in any other way, but also because the class overthrowing it can only in a revolution succeed in ridding itself of all the muck of ages and become fitted to found society anew. .

This is pertinent to a reading of Marxist literary aesthetics because it creates the conditions whereby, as I shall argue that communism will be 'a society of men - artists,' in which the artificial divide between mental and physical labour will be overcome, transcended.

Marx's perspective on ancient Greece and its culture is pertinent to my analysis, here partly because it appears to contradict Reflectionist models and therefore illustrates a diversity of thinking in the two founders of scientific socialism, Marx, and Engels:

A man cannot become a child again unless he becomes childish [....] But the Greeks were normal children. The charm their art has for us does not stand in contradiction with the undeveloped stage of the social order from which it had sprung. It is much more the result of the latter, and separately connected with the circumstance that the unripe social conditions under which the art arose and under which alone it could appear can never return.

Even so we can see a nascent basis for Trotsky's contribution of 'uneven and combined development' to Marxist theory in Marx's theory of ancient Greek culture and society, for Trotsky had realised that history does not develop in a determinist or fatalist manner. Different spheres can progress at an alternative pace while being dialectically linked. Lukacs developed a sophisticated theory of historical materialism that can be compared to Leon Trotsky as in Trotsky's analysis of Dante's Divine Comedy which is comprehended as being more than the product of a historically determined fourteenth-century Florentine but addresses humanity throughout History as being profoundly about the fear of death. . Therefore, we can understand that Trotsky's significant contribution was to the autonomy of art. However, as

bureaucratic counter-revolution was gaining momentum, Trotsky used the term 'fellow traveller' to protect those writers outside of the Party. Both Trotsky and Lukacs understood that the proletariat is not a mechanical cog turned by a giant wheel of history. Instead, Lukacs argued: 'The class consciousness of the proletariat does not develop uniformly throughout the proletariat, parallel to the economic crisis.' Lukacs illustrated the progression from Kant's individualism and Hegel's dialectics to the universality of the proletariat.

Lukacs's synthesis of literary criticism and philosophy is of important because they form a totality with the philosophy expressed in his History and Class Consciousness and Lenin: A Study in The Unity of His Thought. The same narrative of a 'de-reified' and totalised proletariat is applied to literature. He employs the ideas of critical realism as a method of distancing himself from the excesses of the 1934 Writers Congress in the U.S.S.R. with its call for a 'Socialist Realism' as modelled on Maxim Gorky's novel Mother. Rather, Lukacs's view of this form of critical realism understands both the temporal reality and the contradictions of the epoch it describes. However, according to Lukacs, critical realism lacks the world-historic overview of Marxism. Lukacs argued that simply using the form and content of socialist realism is inadequate. He criticises the Stalinist orthodoxy of the period by appealing to both Marx and Lenin as a defence: – despite its ideological difficulties Lukács argued that 'It is no accident that Lenin, like Marx, should regard Tolstoy's realism despite its shortcomings -– as a model of the literature of the future.' .

Thus, I return to one of the founders of scientific socialism, Engels, and his advances in a theory of realist literature after the death of Marx.: Here Engels in a letter to Franz Mehring, 14 July 1893:

Otherwise, there is only one point lacking, which, however, Marx and I always failed to stress enough in our writings and with which we are all equally guilty. That is to say, we all laid, and were bound to lay, the main emphasis, in the first place, on the derivation of political, juridical and other ideological notions, and of actions arising through the medium of these notions, from basic economic facts. But in so doing we neglected the formal side—the ways and means by which these notions, etc., come about—for the sake of the content. [...]In connection with this is the fatuous notion of the ideologist that because we deny an independent historical development to the various ideological spheres which play a part in history, we also deny them any effect upon history. The basis of this is the common undialectical conception of cause and effect as rigidly opposite poles, the total disregarding of interaction. These gentlemen often (almost deliberately) forget that once a historic element has been brought into the world by other, ultimately economic causes, it reacts, can react on its environment and even on the causes that have given rise to it. .

Hence Engels was the first to develop a dialectical Reflectionist theory of aesthetics. Thus, we understand a substantial move forward in literary aesthetics: namely the application of the dialectic to that field.

Therefore, Marx and Engels, as well as the insights of Trotsky, Lukacs and the theoretical models of Victor Serge, Ernst Bloch, and Theodor W. Adorno, will be applied to the three novels under consideration. In the case of Turgenev, we can perceive the first stirrings of the Russian revolutions, an ambiguous manifestation of the model of the 'new man.' However, in the case of Serge's Conquered City's theoretical writings, I shall understand that I would propose using his phrase regarding the novel that it was as being symptomatic of 'defeat-in-victory.' The subjectivism of Bloch 's defence of Expressionism and eventual embracing of messianism in, for instance, Atheism in Christianity are essentially forms of subjective and objective Idealism. This malady, an exacerbated form of abstract defeatism, anticipates in some the genre of 'Weird fiction,' of which it is also in Marxist clothes, as understood in the work of China Melville's 's The City and The

 City. See, for example, it's supposed Marxist aesthetic revealed, as expressed Melville's pessimistic view in his journal, an incongruent pessimism:

Salvage recognizes that the catastrophe is already upon us and that the decisive struggle is over what to do with the remains. Home - Salvage (accessed 03/12/2023) .

'Salvage' is a Marxist art and literature journal founded by China Miéville and others upon his resignation from the unorthodox Trotskyist organisation, the Socialist Workers Party. Given the constraints and contradictions within capitalism as delineated by Marx in 1848:

At a certain stage of development, the material productive forces of society come into contradiction with the existing relations of production. From forms of development of the productive forces these relations turn into their fetters. .

It is therefore possible to perceive some miscomprehension of the Marxist project in Salvage. Marx was neither an economic determinist or a reductionist and he suggests, not that Socialism is inevitable but the conditions in which if both the objective and subjective conditions are

favourable for a proletarian insurrection will succeed and then the circumstances for a new working-class aesthetic will arise. As Trotsky argued in Literature and Revolution (1924), for the full maturing of the masses under the conditions of Socialism. Only then, quoting according to Trotsky (1924):
the average human type will rise to the heights of an Aristotle, a Goethe, or a Marx. And above this ridge, new peaks will rise.
Ultimately, under Socialism, artistic production will be de-alienated labour. A synthesis of physical and mental labour as argued by Adolfo Sanchez Vazquez, who says that 'Marx and Engels conceived of a society of men-artists [..] In communist
society, therefore, every man will be a creator, an artist.' . Thus, under communism, the proletariat will solve the problem posed by Kant as a bourgeois individualist question, i.e., the 'subject-object problem,' and in Lukacs's phrase, will be resolved by the proletariat as an 'identical-subject-object,' a synthesis, a totality, and a universality. For as Lukács explains in History and Class Consciousness: 'But reality can be seized and penetrated only as a totality, and only a subject which itself is a totality is capable of this penetration.' . And he continues persuasively because the proletariat is the universal class. The only class capable of restoring revolutionary literary Realism which the bourgeoisie had established, but as he argued, retreated from after its defeats in the revolutions of 1848. Only the proletariat after a victorious revolution can re-establish the Realist tradition ending what Walter Benjamin had maintained, 'There is no document of culture that is not at the same time a document of barbarism. - Walter Benjamin, "Theses on the Philosophy of History". Hence Lukacs argued:
The proletariat cannot liberate itself as a class without simultaneously abolishing class society as such. For that reason, its consciousness, the last class consciousness in the history of mankind, must both lay bare the nature of society and achieve an increasingly inward fusion of theory and practice. .

Lukács in a later text, The Meaning of Contemporary Realism argues correctly, in my view:
Marx formulated the duty of the revolutionary working-class as follows: 'The class is not concerned about ideals into practice. Its business is to bring to birth those new elements in the womb of decaying bourgeois society.' Lukacs continues' It is no accident that Marx should have opposed romanticism and held Shakespeare and Balzac, the 'cruelly' critical realists, to be the masters of post-classical literature.

Here we can understand Lukacs reemphasising the necessity for literary Realism. Pual Samiran Kumar encapsulates my position eloquently:

If The Theory of the Novel laments the loss of a meaningful human community (represented by ancient Greece), or human society as a 'totality,' Lukacs's great work in Marxist philosophy, History and Class Consciousness (1922), finds this totality in the communist revolution. The communist revolution gives the world back to humanity. The world is once again meaningful, and the Communist Party is then credited with the task of leading the proletariat to its destiny as — in Hegelian terminology – the subject-object of history.
    Finally, I will examine John Molyneux's recent contribution to Marxist aesthetics The Dialectics of Art which I shall argue was ground-breaking. He argued that literary production was ''non-alienated labour' in combination with artistic form and content but which can only find mass fulfilment under socialism and, ultimately, its highest manifestation, communism.   .
This dissertation will explore continuities and discontinuities in Marxist Literary Aesthetics concerning my chosen novels.

Chapter Two: Ivan Turgenev as a Realist novelist and Bazanov as a failed revolutionary in Fathers and Sons? Or a bifurcation between Turgenev's concepts of Hamlet and Don Quixote?
I shall examine the nature of bourgeois or pre-revolutionary literature in this chapter generally, and Turgenev's Fathers

and Sons in particular. Turgenev's novel polarised Russian society. Firstly the 'Fathers' or 'men of the 1840s' whom could be understood as Liberals looking to the West for inspiration of whom Turgenev was inclined towards thought the novel to be unnecessarily sympathetic to the nihilists or 'men of the 1860's'. The 'Sons' or the radical nihilists of the 1860's believed that Turgenev's characterization of Bazarov to be little more than a caricature. Nevertheless, the novel firmly established Turgenev as a leading realist novelist and the Russian realist novel as a major genre. However, to arrive at a more substantial understanding of Turgenev's novel I will return to the methodology established in the introduction and explore Turgenev's speech and an essay written as a prelude to the novel Fathers and Sons, Hamlet, and Don Quixote.

Therefore, following Engels I am interested in 'typicality' in prose-fiction. Lukács elaborated thus on the notion of typicality in Writer and Critic:
The type, according to Marx and Engels, is not the abstract type of classical tragedy, nor the idealized universality as in Schiller, still less what Zola . . . made of it: the average. What characterizes the type is the convergence and intersection of all the dominant aspects of that dynamic unity—all the most important social, moral, and spiritual contradictions of a time. The representation of the average, on the other hand, inevitably results in diluting and deadening these contradictions, the reflection of the great problems of any age.
Here we can ascertain Lukács developing the position initially constructed by Engels in his letter to Margret Hargest on types and typicality in Realism as discussed in the introduction of this dissertation. For Lukács, this typicality relied on inverted Hegelian dialectics, Marx's 'turning these on their head,' Weberian concepts of ideal types and his synthesis of alienation and commodity fetishism which is called reification. The latter taking on a pervasive commodity form which dominates much of the globe. Although, alternatively, Lenin had argued 'Capitalism has triumphed all

over the world, but this triumph is only the prelude to the triumph of labour over capital..'

Lukács in Writer and Critic further embellishes these ideas and illustrates how the parts of a realist novel combine to create its totality and typicality:
the novel provides the effect of a terrifyingly accurate and typical picture of bourgeois society. . ... The effect itself results from the composition, from the context provided by the relationships of the extreme cases, a context in which the apparent outlandishness of the individual cases is eliminated. Extract any one of the conflicts from the general context and you discover fantastic, melodramatic, improbable tale. But . . . through the piling up of extreme cases . . . an atmosphere arises which eliminates any sense of their being extreme and improbable . . . in which the social reality of capitalist society emerges . . . in a crassness and fullness that could not otherwise be realized.

Lukács here is illustrating the rational mechanism from which the totality of the novel is constructed. However, as I had shown in the previous introductory chapter Lukács believed the Realist novel to be in decline, after establishing itself in early capitalism following the failure of the bourgeois revolutions of 1848 with the bourgeoisie descending into reaction both artistically and politically.

Trotsky, however maintained an alternative position on which he was absolutely clear in regards of pre-revolutionary literature:
Having broken up human relations into atoms, bourgeois society, had a great aim for itself. Personal emancipation was its name. In reality, all modern literature has been nothing but an enlargement of this theme.

Leon Trotsky wrote this in 1924 in the early days of the Russian revolution. There had been an outpouring of artistic energy and experimentation before the bureaucratic counter-revolution and Trotsky's writings and speeches on literature and art reflected this. However, Georgi Lukács had understood in The Theory of the Novel that 'Turgenev— was

an essentially a Western European novelist of disillusionment.' Lenin wrote rather more caustically when Chernyshevsky was arrested, (the author of What is to be Done) that many of the Liberal writers such as:
'The vile liberal Kaveliin wrote: 'I see nothing shocking in these arrests...the revolutionary party considers all means fair to overthrow the government, and the latter defends itself by its own means...The liberal Turgenev wrote a private letter to Tsar Alexander II assuring him of his loyalty and donated two gold pieces for the soldiers wounded in the suppression of the Polish insurrection.
.
Hence, it is possible to ascertain that the reception of Turgenev generally in Trotsky, and particularly of Lukács and Lenin was not entirely positive. Although, we can understand that Lenin was not the dogmatic ideologue portrayed in much literature about him published in the previous Stalinist states. I contrast the complexity of Lenin's thought as Frederik Jameson quotes him devastatingly:
'Intelligent idealism is closer to intelligent materialism than unintelligent materialism.

Emma Goldman, the anarchist thinker, and activist, took a more constructive and even positive view of Turgenev's Fathers and Sons, thus:
It may in a measure be compared to the early period of the awakening of the Russian intellectuals described by Turgenev in "Fathers and Sons. The intellectuals of that time, while never so superficial as those I am talking about, indulged in revolutionary ideas, split hairs through the early morning hours, philosophized about all sorts of questions and carried their superior wisdom to the people with their feet deeply rooted in the old. Of course they failed. They were indignant with Turgenev and considered him a traitor to Russia. But he was right. Only when the Russian intellectuals completely broke with their traditions; only when they fully realized that society rests upon a lie, and that they must give themselves to the new completely and unreservedly, did they become a forceful factor in the life of the people. The Kropotkin's, the Perovskayas, the

Breshkovskayas, and hosts of others repudiated wealth and station and refused to serve King Mammon.

Her position was consistent with the life of unremitting activism and commitment she lived e.g. the assassination attempt with Alexander Berkman of the bourgeois Frick during a particularly intense industrial dispute in 1892. She was at that time a Bakuninist and, therefore, believed in 'propaganda by deed.' Thus, a lineage with the nihilist/Narodnik can be discerned if not quite a continuity as we can ascertain in this passage in Fathers and Sons
"What is Bazanov?" Arcady smiled. "Would you like me to tell you, uncle, what he really is?"
"Please do, nephew."
"He is a nihilist!"
"What?" asked Nikolai Petrovich, while Pavel Petrovich lifted his knife in the air with a small piece of butter on the tip and remained motionless.
"He is a nihilist," repeated Arkady.
"A nihilist," said Nikolai Petrovich. "That comes from the Latin nihil, nothing, as far as I can judge; the word must mean a man who... who recognizes nothing?"
"Say — who respects nothing," interposed Pavel Petrovich and lowered his knife with the butter on it.
"Who regards everything from the critical point of view," said Arkady.
"Isn't that exactly the same thing?" asked Pavel Petrovich.
"No, it's not the same thing. A nihilist is a person who does not bow down to any authority, who does not accept any principle on faith, however much that principle may be revered."
"Well and is that good?" asked Pavel Petrovich. "That depends, uncle dear. For
some it is good, for others very bad."
"Indeed. Well, I see that's not in our line. We old-fashioned people think that without principles, taken as you say on faith, one can't take a step or even breathe. Voss ages change tout cela; may God grant you health and a general's

rank, and we shall be content to look on and admire your... what was the name?"
"Nihilists," said Arcady, pronouncing very distinctly.
"Yes, there used to be Hegelists and now there are nihilists. We shall see how you will manage to exist in the empty airless void; and now ring, please, brother Nikolai, it's time for me to drink my cocoa.' .

Turgenev employs the third-person omniscient view throughout the novel but with dazzling exchanges of dialogue as in this example. This interaction encapsulates the dialectical polarisation between the generations and their perspectives. However, Turgenev was not writing with the same intent as Maxim Gorky i.e. he was 'showing' not 'telling.' Another way of articulating this is that Turgenev wrote with more authorial distance. He was writing, indeed developing the realist genre rather than the socialist realist one adopted in 1934 at the Soviet Writers Congress as the matrix for all Leftist writing. Although, as I have shown both Trotsky and Serge opposed this manoeuvre. I have argued that it was the product of the bureaucratic counter-revolution which was firmly established with the expulsion of Trotsky from the USSR in 1929 and taken to a bloody conclusion with the Moscow Show Trials in the mid-1930s and concluded with Trotsky's assassination in 1940. For the historical materialist you cannot abstract literary production from its sociocultural, indeed, socio-economic foundations. Recollecting Engels letter (1888) to Mehring ideological phenomena once created by economic factors can have a dialectical interaction with the socio-economic base. The Marxist method is neither reductionist or 'vulgar' when not distorted by either counter-revolutionary elements or bourgeois ideologues.

However, Irina N. Sizemskya argued:
Turgenev called himself a realist, and was incredulous of all systems and
absolutes. The writer, he believed, should not prove anything or pass

judgment on his characters. He was interested in the living truth of life
and believed that realism was the product of a faith based on knowledge,
which a person receives from reason and not divine grace. His work
reflected the truths and delusions of the main European and Russian sociophilosophical ideas of the second half of the nineteenth century—
scepticism and positivism, Westernism and Slavophilism…liberalism and conservatism, Marxism, and liberal radicalism. From the early 1860s, nihilism held a special place in the public imagination. This is not accidental. At the time, Russian culture was consumed by social, political, and civil protest, by the search for new meanings of life. The history of Russian nihilism began earlier with N.I. Nadezhda's article, "The Crowd of Nihilists" (1829), in which he criticized writers who he believed were straying from the classical tradition.
After becoming part of the radical youth world view, it acquired the maximalist idea of "strike right, strike left, this will not make things worse, it cannot" (Dmitry Piyare) …. It can be said that it was affirmed in Russian social thought as a synthesis of positivism, individualism, and socioethical utopianism. It was this nihilism that intrigued Turgenev. The theme of nihilism is sometimes exclusively associated with Fathers and Sons. However, although the theme of nihilism is central to the novel, the questions it raises are prevalent throughout Turgenev's work. .

Thus, we can examine another sphere in Turgenev, the Realist novel in an epoch of revolutionary ferment. The significant claims of Richard Freeborn is that the mid-nineteenth century Russian novel had become a vehicle for the revolutionary debates which were taking place in the literary 'thick journals' of the time. Thus, making them central to the social and literary discourse and, I would argue, interacting dialectically between those arenas. Another significant contribution of Freeborn's was revealing Stepniak, S., The Career of a Nihilist; a Novel (New York,

Harper & Brothers, 1889) as a third strand in revolutionary Russian literature describing a psychological study of the Nihilist. Interestingly, the latter was written in English. Freeborn locates the Russian revolutionary novel in a position unique to that narrative in three spheres:1) the novels of Turgenev which brought the socio-cultural ideas of the milieu into the mainstream, 2) those like Chernyshevsky, What is to be Done which was written for tendentious purposes and 3) Stepniak, S., The Career of a Nihilist; a Novel that was scribed to provide an insight into the inner life, the psychology, of the Nihilist. This might well be an acute observation but also ignores the revolutionary literature of, for instance, England with the poetry and prose of John Milton regarding the first bourgeois revolution, the English Revolution.

Freeborn continues:

The Russian novel became the midwife to the revolutionary impulse in Russian society. In turn, it draws inspiration and creative life from that impulse.

Here lies the quintessence of my argument regarding the Russian novel in the period I will examine in this chapter which was the significant moment in politico-cultural questions prior to the revolution and after Turgenev's 'nihilist' novel.

At the International Socialist Congress in Paris in 1889, within six months after the appearance of Stepniak's novel, Plekhanov declared:
The task of our revolutionary intellectuals…amounts, in the opinion of the Russian Social Democrats, to the following: they must master the views of modern scientific socialism spread them amongst the workers, with the help of the workers, take by assault the citadel of autocracy. The revolutionary movement in Russia can triumph only as the revolutionary movement of the workers. There is not and cannot be any other way out for us.

Freeborn importantly locates the moment Sergei Plekhanov, and the nascent Russian Marxist movement, rejected the acts of individual violence by the Nihilists/Narodniks in favour of a collective proletarian revolution. He does this successfully in the context of Russian literature. This is pertinent to my argument because as Leon Trotsky remarked in Literature and Revolution (1924) that "there are many people in this world who think as revolutionaries and feel as philistines.

However, the Russian Social Democrats did not doubt the courage of the nihilists/Narodniks but their 'turn' to the peasantry in the 1860s could never produce socialism because of its lack of collectivity. Indeed, Lenin's older brother was executed for his involvement with the nihilist/Narodniks. It was only when the emergent proletariat begun to develop with a stratum of disaffected intelligentsia committed to scientific socialism in that the potential arose for a reconfiguration of social relations became possible. Herein lies an inadequate trait in Bazanov as neither the objective nor subjective conditions for his nihilism existed. Nevertheless, Marx and Engels Preface to the Russian edition of the Communist Manifesto did suggest an interesting view of the obshchina (village commune) which the nihilist/Narodniks had understood as the primary structure for socialism in Russia. Of course, this predates the soviets or workers councils established by proletarians firstly in 1905 during the first Worker's revolution. Rather though Marx and Engels provided an intriguing perspective for the movement and its later influence that was emergent in 1862 when Turgenev wrote Fathers and Sons. They speculate on the obshchina or village commune as a potential model for socialism. Again, this illustrates the lack of dogmatism in their thinking but also the influence of the Narodniks on radical thought, even in the West. Bazarov was not an isolated figment of literary discourse and nor can he have been in the context of an authentic Marxist argument:

But in Russia we find, face-to-face with the rapidly flowering capitalist swindle and bourgeois property, just beginning to develop, more than half the land owned in common by the peasants.

Now the question is: can the Russian obshchina, though greatly undermined, yet a form of primeval common ownership of land, pass directly to the higher form of Communist common ownership? Or, on the contrary, must it first pass through the same process of dissolution such as constitutes the historical evolution of the West?

The only answer to that possible today is this: If the Russian Revolution becomes the signal for a proletarian revolution in the West, so that both complement each other, the present Russian common ownership of land may serve as the starting point for a communist development.

Marx and Engels were engaged in literary as well as ideological spheres of their milieu, thus being consistent with their methodology as illustrated by S. S. Prawler Marx and World Literature in which Prawler illustrates the diversity of their involvement with literature.

I note Turgenev's speech of 1860 entitled and then published the same year as Hamlet and Don Quixote in which he argued there were two essential 'types' in humanity and, therefore, realist literature: Hamlets and Don Quixotes:

Do not all men belong more or less to one type or the other? Does not each one of us side either with Don Quixote or with Hamlet? Today Hamlets outnumber Don Quixotes, though Quixotes are to be found.

This is significant in that he expounded these ideas in 1860 two years before the publication of Fathers and Sons. As A. V. Knowles noted that in 1860 in an article published in The Contemporary Turgenev views on the two human and thus literary types: Hamlets and Don Quixotes. He describes the former as 'Hamlet is a more reflective type, more subtle more of the philosopher.... [but] he cannot do anything because of indecision, doubt, and intellectualizing.' Knowles argues that the Hamlet types first reference was in a letter to the woman who was Turgenev's major romantic interest,

Pauline Viaduct in a Letter of 25th December 1847. Don
Quixotes 'in contrast 'act on impulse, never worrying about
the consequences of his actions.' For Turgenev both are
meek and are embodied in his perception of the Russian
peasantry, Knowles argues. However, it is necessary to
comprehend the characters major protagonists in Fathers
and Sons as, contrary to Knowles' viewpoint contradicting
these two '. Rather, they represent the established yet
aspiring rural gentry on the one hand and the disaffected
rising young intelligentsia on the other; Fathers and Sons.

Finally, I argue Bazanov failed as a revolutionary
because he was broken by his unrequited love for a
widowed Countess, Anna Sergeyevna Odintsova. Although
she too had progressive ideas, they did not entertain a
romance, maybe more, with a medical student from, in
comparison meagre means. Also, perhaps it would have
meant 'praxis'. Although she visits him on his deathbed,
dying of typhus, …

Well, goodbye! Live a long life, that's best of all, and enjoy it
while there's time. You can see what an ugly spectacle I am,
a half-crushed worm and still

showing off. And I used to think, after all, I'll do a whole
mass of things, I'll not

die, no way! There's a task to be done and I'm a giant! And
now the giant's only task is to die decently, although no one
cares a damn about that… '

The novel ends with multiple nuclear marriages. Not quite
what Alexandra Kollontai would envisage for the fledging
Bolshevik states in her article Communism and the Family
Communism and the Family by Alexandra Kollontai -
Marxists Internet Archive . A new configuration of the
decaying relationships of bourgeois society. So, in answer to
my rhetorical question was Bazanov 'a failed revolutionary?'
Yes because, in the last instant, he was not part of a totality,
an 'identical-subject-object,' the proletariat as argued in the
introduction. If Bazanov was a Hamlet or a Don Quixote? If
he was moulded from those characters, I argue, that was a
limitation and his future lay only as 'New Man.' As does
humanity's destiny.

Chapter Three.
**Victor Serge Conquered City: a tale of contradictory
beliefs and times.**

Victor Serge was an author of novels and political literature.
His life was defined by the moment the Russian proletariat
seized state power in October 1917 as described by David
Cotterall:
For Victor Serge, as for many of his contemporaries, the
Russian Revolution marked a turning point in his political life.
It forced upon him a major shift in his political allegiances, a
break with previous affiliations and the adoption of a new
political theory and practice, revolutionary Marxism, to which
he had hitherto been deeply hostile.

I shall argue that in his trilogy of novels: Firstly, Men in
Prison, secondly, Birth of our Power and thirdly, Conquered
City. Although these novels are not precisely
autobiographical, they are what Richard Greeman termed
'witness novels' in that they pay 'witness' to three major
phases in Serge's life. Greeman developed this concept into
'the martyr-witness, he argues that 'Victor Serge was such a
martyr- witness.'i Hence the first novel, Men in Prison was
about his imprisonment in France for refusing to inform on a
group of Bakuninist anarchists who had been bombing and
robbing banks in Paris in 1912. Serge was an anarchist of
that persuasion in that period and wrote under the penname
The Awkward Customer. He was incarcerated for five years
between 1912-1917. Secondly, Birth of our Power illustrated
his movement away from atomised individualist anarchism to
anarcho- syndicalism and an embracing of the proletariat as
the agent of social transformation. Thirdly, Conquered City
delineated his arrival in Petrograd in 1919 at a time of hope
yet jeopardy for the Bolshevik revolution. My argument will
sustain David Cottrell's position as articulated by Ian
Birchall:
But the bleakness of the context did not blunt the polemic
between Serge and Trotsky; on the contrary it made them

both more determined to fight for the ideas they believed could offer a way out. David Cotterill tries to identify roots of the differences between the two men as lying in their political origins, arguing that whilst Trotsky's views were formed 'within the Russian movement,' Serge's were 'imbued with the experience of Western movements' .

Therefore, there is an aspect of ideological inconsistency in Serge's position in comparison to the systematic perspective of Trotsky. Serge attempted to resolve the contradiction between his previous anarchist affinities and Bolshevism until his death in 1947 but, I suggest never succeeded in achieving a synthesis. While Trotsky retained a Marxist method until his murder in 1940 at the hands of a Stalinist agent. However, both Serge and Trotsky opposed the degeneration of the revolution with allegiance to the Left Opposition.

Thus, I will argue three positions. That anarchism and Marxism are, in the last instance irreconcilable in that the former renounces the seizure of state power and the latter the establishment of a worker's state or the dictatorship of the proletariat. The state as Engels argued 'withering away' once the higher state of communism had developed. Secondly, that the writing of Conquered City in the shadow of the counter-revolution in 1932 should be compared with his writing of the period in defence of the fledgling but endangered workers state Serge Revolution in Danger writings from Russia 1919-1921. . Serge was writing Conquered City in what he had described as the 'midnight of the century.' His wife driven insane by the constant harassment and persecution and comrades disappearing. This was the logical yet ruthless consequence of the defeat of the international revolutionary movement and the triumph of Stalin's policy of 'socialism in one country.' It is against this socio- historical backdrop that the novel and the debates must be understood. Finally, I will suggest that the text of Conquered City is profoundly ambiguous; it 'tells' one narrative and 'shows' others. This is, I argue, symptomatic of the profound contradictions with Serge's ideological adherences. Let me provide one example in that Serge was the only leading member of the Bolshevik leadership to attend the funeral of the Anarchist philosopher Peter Kropotkin in 1921. Ian Birchall continues:

Serge's ambivalence was rooted in the very real contradictions of the revolution. For a revolution fighting for its very life, the terror and such instruments as the Cheka were a necessity. That does not require us to deny that specific actions of the Cheka manifested incompetence, overzealous sectarianism, and pure vindictiveness. Serge knew that unless he compromised with Bolshevism, he would be condemned to moralizing impotence. Yet it was a real compromise, and it entailed contradictions that were not always easy to handle. Serge himself later formulated the problem in terms of what he called the "double duty" of the revolutionary, who must defend the revolution against both its external enemies and its own internal weaknesses. So, it is not surprising that a number of those who knew Serge during the early years of the revolution—the anarchists Gaston Level and Mauricius, or the French communist Marcel Body who worked closely with Serge—testify to the fact that while his writings were solidly in support of the revolution, in private conversation with those he thought he could trust he made sharp criticisms of the Bolshevik regime. Level quotes him as saying: "We are obliged to lie to save what can be saved of the revolution."

In comparison Trotsky wrote:

The proletarian dictatorship is just a bridge between the bourgeois and the socialist society. In its very essence, therefore, it bears a temporary character. An incidental but very essential task of the state which realizes the dictatorship consists in preparing for its own dissolution. The degree of the realization of this "incidental" task is, to some extent, a measure of its success in the fulfilment of its fundamental mission: the construction of a society without classes and without material contradictions. Bureaucracy and social harmony are inversely proportional to each other. In his famous polemic against Duhring, Engels wrote:

"When, together with class domination and the struggle for individual existence created by the present anarchy in production, those conflicts and excesses which result from this struggle disappear, from that time on there will be nothing to suppress, and there will be no need for a special instrument of suppression, the state.

So, on initial reading the two revolutionaries shared a similar position. However, Serge believed 'the germ of Stalinism was in Bolshevism' which led him to reject Trotsky's founding of the Fourth International in 1938. The latter being founded on Bolshevik organizational principles.

To return to my close reading of Conquered City it was a novel both employing conventional prose techniques for example Serge uses a 'framing device' with a young Cheka woman writing a poem:

Revolution: Fire

Burn out the man of old. Burn yourself. Man's renewal by fire.

She held her twenty-year-old head in her hands as she sat pensive over these lines.

Regeneration of man through the red-hot iron. Plow up the old earth, tear down the old structure. Recreate life anew. And in all likelihood perish yourself. I will perish. Man will live. Yet still a dull anxiety. Is that too the man of old resisting? Victory, smile into the void: Very well, I'll perish, I'm ready. .

Her male comrade overhears and replies: "Writing, Xenia?"

"Oh, it's you!"

Without any surprise, not even turning all the way around, she nodded at the lines she had just scrawled.

"Read it, Ryjik. And tell me if it's all right."

"Burn out the man of old. Burn   "

Ryjik straightened up, totally subdued.

"All right? All right? I don't know. I don't like romanticism. Empty phases. Everything is much simpler: Imperialism, class war, dictatorship, proletarian consciousness ... See you tomorrow." .

Here Serge is beginning the narrative with a comparison between the idealist and the stolid revolutionary which recurs throughout the novel. The recurring phrase from both personifications of the Cheka is 'It was necessary.' On the penultimate page the author returns to the opening passage about Xenia and Ryjik. Amidst the Red and White Terror at the beginning and conclusion of the novel we are told two very human stories, those of Xenia and Ryjik. Serge had to smuggle out the manuscript in sections which might account for some of the fragmentation. However, although written in 1930-31, three years before the Writers Congress, 1934 it is possible perceive Serge moving towards modernism and away from conventional realism while maintaining some conventional methods like this 'framing device' beginning on page 6 and here concluding at page 184:

"Hello, Ryzhik? That you, Ryzhik? Raid over; picked up three bundles of letters and documents; seized twelve pounds of butter, seventy pounds of floor, two dozen cakes of soap…. Wait a minute, what else, yes, photos, and cans, eighteen of them… - No, no arrests. The bastards flew the coop. they fired a few shots…. - Xenia/ Xenia got two bullets in the belly…" These last two words took on their full meaning in his mind only slowly. They exploded and went out. They lit up again in the depth of his consciousness like the little blue safety lamps in boiler rooms which sometimes indicate that the pressure has gotten too high; danger – then there was the carnal image of a wounded belly. Ryzhik went down to the library. His jaw was rigid, his eyes vague.
Two soldiers were chatting by the light of a night lamp next to the big Dutch earthenware stove.
Ryzhik, his back against the stove to let the heat penetrate him, closed his eyes. The night reigned, magnificently silent, over the snow, the ice, the city.
"You look awful, Ryzhik," said one of the men.
Serge 'shows' in the context of the tales of two Cheka agents both the love and suffering of the conquered Conquered City. It is the dialogue between the individual and the collective.
Trotsky, in 1937, provided a cogent position on the nature of the transition to communism:

It is true that capitalist anarchy creates the struggle of each against all, but the trouble is that a socialization of the means of production does not yet automatically remove the "struggle for individual existence." That is the nub of the question!

The proletariat, the Cheka and the Red Army defeated the counter-revolutionary forces including foreign armed groups as well as British military forces. But at a huge price with Lenin describing the USSR as a 'bureaucratically distorted workers state' in 1922. As Engels had argued in the letter to Mehring quoted in the introduction there can be dialectical interaction between the base and the superstructure. This was the case with literature on the Left. As the revolutionary forces were retreating

in Russia with the defeats of the German, Hungarian and Italian revolutions between 1919-1922 the drift towards defending the new ruling bureaucracy was palpably triumphing in the 1934 Writers Congress and the adaptation of Socialist Realism as the hegemonic form. Serge anticipated this position in Conquered City and his phrase in regards of the novel as 'defeat in victory.' However, this does not explain some of the self-inflicted wounds in the novel. It is not a novel, I suggest, that a Trotskyist would have written. Some of it is harrowing beyond description. There is a difference between critiquing creatively errors and writing about the rape of a child.

This can only be explained by Serge's ideological contradictions i.e. between anarchism and Marxism. His inability to reconcile the petty bourgeois tendencies of his pre-1919 orientation which when compounded by the establishment of Stalinism as a political force, he fell into fictional laceration rather than creative fictional criticism. This is not to diminish Serge's achievements but to differentiate them from Trotsky's contributions with the thinkers moving further apart e.g. disagreements over both the POUM in the Spanish Civil War and the foundation of the Fourth International in 1938.

To contrast the convoluted narrative of Conquered City delineated with the revolutionary fervour of Serge's journey to and arrival in Petrograd is quite stunning. From the scenes of abomination described in Conquered City which begun as he wrote in his earlier text Revolution in Danger: writings from Russia 1919-1922:

We felt as if we were leaving the void and entering the kingdom of the will [...] A land awaited us where life was beginning anew, where conscious will, intelligence and an inexorable love of mankind were in action. Behind us, all Europe was ablaze, having choked almost to death in the fog of its own massacres. Barcelona's flame smouldered on. Germany was in the thick of revolution, Austro-Hungary was splitting into free nations. Italy was spread with red flags [...]

This was only the beginning

Some corrective words from Vsievolod Volkov, an orthodox Trotskyist, provide us with the context and orientation to comprehend the nature of the circumstances. Unlike Serge's Conquered City this is not ambiguous with the contradictory 'double duty' which was in reality a misunderstanding of these circumstances; the germ of Stalinism did not lie in Bolshevism.

Neither Marx nor Engels, neither Lenin nor Trotsky can be made responsible for the twisting and falsification of the theories of revolutionary Marxism in order to justify the oppression and subjugation of the working class by a privileged bureaucratic caste, which ended up by annihilating the first triumphant socialist revolution on the planet. .

Therefore, the roots of the counter-revolutionary bureaucracy were not innate within revolutionary socialism as argued by Victor Serge and 'shown' in his novel Conquered City in horrific detail but rather lay in external factors. We see Serge's departure from critical realism as symptomatic of his position. Thus, we can discern the dialectical relationship between base and superstructure, society and literature as delineated by Engels in his letter to Mehring quoted in the introduction. 14. Therefore, the concrete conditions of Petrograd were not merely reflected in the superstructure arena of the writing of Serge. They in turn interactively reacted on the literary production of the three 'witness novels.'ii

Chapter Four.
China Melville's The City and The City: the defeat of a revolution and the death of a genre.

My argument has been that the defeat of the October revolution and the counter- revolutionary revenge of the Stalinist bureaucracy transformed the Zeitgeist of modern humanity. Therefore, inevitably, its impact on both literary production and philosophy was immense. Like Trotsky I would argue that this was not inevitable and the potential for socialist revolution and its ramifications for literature and humanity remain. I think Lukacs encapsulated the argument in History and Class Consciousness for the continuing relevance of Marxism. Lukacs asked What is Orthodox Marxism?

THIS question, simple as it is, has been the focus of much discussion in both proletarian and bourgeois circles…Let us assume for the sake of argument that recent research had disproved once and for all every one of Marx's individual theses. Even if this were to be proved, every serious unorthodox Marxist would still be able to accept all such modern findings without reservation and hence dismiss all of Marx's theses in toto ± without having to renounce his orthodoxy for a single moment. Orthodox Marxism, therefore, does not imply the uncritical acceptance of the results of Marx's investigations. It is not the µbelief' in this or that thesis, nor the exegesis of a µsacred' book. On the contrary, orthodoxy refers exclusively to method. It is the scientific conviction that dialectical materialism is the road to truth and that its methods can be developed, expanded, and deepened only along the lines laid down by its founders. It is the conviction, moreover, that all attempts to surpass or µimprove' it has led and must lead to over-simplification, triviality, and eclecticism.

Thus, the nature of Marxism is, in the last instance, in its methodology and that method is a living tradition, a burning flame no matter how dark the night. There have been Marxists who believed the catastrophes of Stalinism,

Fascism and then the mass commodification and reification of considerable sections of humanity meant the impossibility of the worker's revolution. One of which was Theodor W. Adorno. He argued regarding the novel:

If the novel wishes to remain true to its realist foundations and say how things really are, it has to repudiate a realism which, by producing a facade, only helps to foster a trade in deception.

Another response was posited by Ernst Bloch in which he firstly turned to subjectivism in form of utopian speculation and then a form of messianism which he attempted to fuse the ideas of the 16th century apocalyptic teacher Thomas Munster with Marxism. These ideas were, as I argued in the introduction, forms of subjective and objective Idealism in contrast with Dialectical Materialism. However, consistently with my methodology and argument I reject Adorno's pessimism and Bloch's Idealism. Although a position in the unorthodox Trotskyist magazine Socialist Review maintained Gareth Jenkins from Socialist Review says that Bloch "argues that there are liberatory, 'atheist' elements within Christianity with which socialists should make common cause."

The City and The City concludes with Raymond Chandler inspired 'hard -boiled' detective Inspector Tyador Borlú totally capitulating and working for Breach.:

is changed: not to uphold the law, or another law, but to maintain the skin that keeps law in place. Two laws in two places, in fact. That is the end of the case of Orciny and the archaeologists, the last case of Inspector Tyador Borlú of the Besel Extreme Crime Squad. Inspector Tyador Borlú is gone. I sign off Tye, avatar of Breach, following my mentor on my probation out of Besel and out of Ul Qoma. We are all philosophers here where I am, and we debate among many other things the question of where it is that we live. On that issue I am a liberal. I live in the interstice yes, but I live in both the city and the city.

As Carl Freedman comments to reinforce this reflection:

The executive – who is, by no means incidentally, the man ultimately most responsible for Mahalia's murder – takes off in his corporate helicopter and escapes scot-free; for the power represented or figured by the helicopters of multinational corporations is, for a miniscule national entity like Besźel or Ul Qoma, irresistible. Beyond the deflationary generic conventions of crime fiction – but by no means unrelated to them – lies the most powerful deflationary force in our world structured by uneven and combined development: the Yankee dollar.

So, although Miéville makes numerous sloganizing comments favourable to the Marxist-Leninist Unificationalists, against fascist grouplets and some excellent points on xenophobia through his device of the seeing and unseeing of the citizens of Besźel or Ul Qoma. Nevertheless, his movement away from proletarian or Realist fiction is curious. Even in The City and The City where 'Weird Fiction' is tempered by the genre of detective fiction it is a class fiction, but not a proletarian genre. Realism as Lukacs and Terry Eagleton (2024) argued was a bourgeois genre but can be appropriated by the masses not as Socialist Realism but as variations on critical realism in the future. We can begin to see further what Lukacs described as 'The Destruction of Reason' . He understood this as the growth of 'irrationalism' as manifest not only in the philosophy of Nietzsche but also in the literature of Joyce and Kafka as factors in the rise of fascism. It is interest to note that Miéville references Kafka. I am not arguing that Miéville is providing oxygen for fascism but what I am arguing is that as a result of the world-historic defeat of the nascent Russian revolution literary production has, inevitably, been affected as elaborated in my positions delineated in this dissertation.
However, as argued by Heraclius, an early dialectical thinker, Πάντα ῥεῖ [Everything flows] δὶς ἐς τὸν αὐτὸν ποταμὸν οὐκ ἂν ἐμβαίης [You cannot step in the same river

twice] —Heraclitus c. 535–c. 475 BCE. . After centuries adrift: "Here we see land", commented Hegel, "there is no proposition of Heraclitus which I have not included in my Logic.' Likewise, Engels in Dialectics of Nature outlines dialectics:

It is, therefore, from the history of nature and human society that the laws of dialectics are abstracted. For they are nothing but the most general laws of these two aspects of historical development, as well as of thought itself. And indeed, they can be reduced in the main to three:

The law of the transformation of quantity into quality and vice versa.

The law of the interpenetration of opposites.

The law of the negation of the negation.

Thus, we can understand both history and matter in motion and propelled by contradiction. Therefore, although I argued in favour of critical realism and was weary of Miéville and the genre and permutations of the genre he writes within here I find some common ground with the author for example please see here:

No matter how commodified the fantastic in its various forms might be, we need fantasy to think the world, and to change it.

Also, Miéville argues:

Real" life under capitalism is a fantasy: "realism," narrowly defined, is, therefore, a "realistic" depiction of "an absurdity which is true" […] but no less absurd for that.

Therefore, a reappraisal of the methodology of the genres of science-fiction and Weird fantasy is required. To this end, I examine the concept introduced by Darko Suvin in Metamorphosis Fiction (1979). In this influential text, he introduced the concept of 'cognitive estrangement.' Essentially Suvin fused two concepts: firstly, defamiliarization or 'making strange' from the Russian Formalists and taking from Bertolt Brecht the idea of the 'alienation effect'. To quote Suvin:

a literary genre whose necessary and sufficient conditions are the presence and interaction of estrangement and cognition, and whose main formal device is an imaginative framework alternative to the author's empirical environment. So, we see an underpinning for, Weird, Miéville's phrase for his fictional output. Weird Fiction,

However, where does this leave Marxist poetics, Lenin was clear that they must be both partisan and proletarian: Literature must become a cog and a screw of one single great social democratic machine.' Neutrality in writing, he argues, is impossible: 'The freedom of the bourgeois writer is only masked dependence on the money bag! … Down with non-partisan writers!' What is needed is a 'broad, multiform, and various literature inseparably linked with the working-class movement

This was written with absolute clarity and created a matrix for pre-revolutionary leftist writing. Lukacs would eloquently elaborate on this theme:

It is no accident that Lenin, like Marx, should regard Tolstoy's realism despite its shortcomings --- as a model of the literature of the future.

Therefore, I am in accord with Lenin on literature and literary commitment and Lukács on the rudimentary generic requirements for socialist literature. Hence, although I see merit in Miéville and Suvin's literary criticism it is only with full-fledged freedom of society after the transition to communism that these experimentations can achieve fruition. For an early Bolshevik utopian novel see Alexander Bogdanov's Red Star.

Hence Miéville's fictional writing is self-evidently both imaginative and intelligent it is a form of Left Reformism in that it does not provide a concrete Marxist perquisite for proletarian revolution. For as Lenin wrote: 'the very gist and soul of Marxism is the concrete analysis of concrete situations.'   Therefore, my inclination is towards Realism rather than Weird Fiction, or other types of the genre

comprising Utopian fiction. My argument is in primary accord with Lukacs:
Lukács's view of the great European realists of the 19th century as essentially bourgeois writers, and he claimed that their   achievements should serve as a guide to proletarian or socialist writers   in the 20th century.

In a proletarian society, the full creative potential of humanity will be released. As Trotsky argued
However, does not an excess of solidarity, as the Nietzscheans fear, threaten to degenerate man into a sentimental, passive, herd animal? Not at all. The powerful force of competition which, in bourgeois society, has the character of market competition, will not disappear in a socialist society, but to use the language of psychoanalysis, will be sublimated, that is, will assume a higher and more fertile form. There will be the struggle for one's opinion, for one's project, for one's taste. In the measure in which political struggles will be eliminated – and in a society where there will be no classes, there will be no such struggles – the liberated passions will be channelled into technique, into construction which also includes art. Art then will become more general, will mature, will become tempered, and will become the most perfect method of the progressive building of life in every field.

As Trotsky argued and I concur in the highest stage of communism every person will become an Aristotle, a Goethe, a Marx, and maybe, I suggest, a Charlotte Bronte or a Sappho. Finally, Melville was not writing in either the pre-revolutionary epoch that Turgenev was or, equally, the post-revolutionary period in which Serge wrote and this is illustrated in his choice of genre and content.

Conclusion: Nineteenth and Twentieth century Russia: a laboratory for literature.

Results and Prospects or continuities and discontinuities?

In answer to the question, I posed: Marxist Literary Aesthetics or continuities and discontinuities in three novels: Ivan Turgenev's Fathers and Sons, Victor Serge's Conquered City and China Miéville's The City and The City? My answer is that there is an unbroken lineage in Western aesthetics and, equally, an unbroken thread in Marxist aesthetics but with deviations in both cases. The source of Marxist literary criticism lies in the dialectical and materialist critique of Western aesthetics and can be understood to have its origins in the young Marx's analysis of Hegel. Therefore, my method of Dialectical and Historical Materialism is applied to literature. This is why I was focused on the early Greek dialectician Heraclitus c. 535–c. 475 BCE i.e. 'You cannot step in the same river twice.' My argument in delineating Western aesthetics and more specially the variations in Marxist aesthetics from Marx and paying particular attention to two late letters from Engels to those who applied the method from Lukacs, Trotsky, Lenin, Bloch, and, marginally, Miéville. The majority of my position has been made. That there was a paradigm shift in the relationship between the base and superstructure, between the relations and forces of production and the ideologies of a society in 1917. Let us examine two passages from Marx: The production of life ... appears as a double relationship: on the one hand as a natural, on the other as a social relationship ... It follows from this that a certain mode of production, or industrial stage, is always combined with a certain mode of co-operation, or social stage, and this mode of co-operation is itself a "productive force." Further, that the multitude of productive forces accessible to men determines the nature of society.

We comprehend the interactive manner of the mode of production and the social nature of production. I have argued that 'labour' is humanity's 'species-being' following the young Marx in Economic and Philosophical Manuscripts of 1844. Again, here in Capital Volume 3:

The specific economic form, in which unpaid surplus-labour is pumped out of direct producers, determines the relationship of rulers, and ruled, as it grows directly out of production itself and, in turn, reacts upon it as a determining element. Upon this, however, is founded the entire formation of the economic community which grows up out of production relations themselves, thereby simultaneously its specific political form. It is always the direct relationship of the owners of the conditions of production to the direct producers
- a relation always naturally corresponding to a definite stage in the development of the methods of labour and thereby its social productivity - which reveals the innermost secret, the hidden basis of the entire social structure.

A number of clear relationships are delineated in this short but dense passage. Firstly, the specific economic form of the expropriation of surplus-labour determines the relationships between rulers and ruled. The formation of the economic community grows up out of these relations of production. The direct relation between owners and producers reveals the foundation of the social structure. These direct relations correspond to a definite state in the development of the methods of labour. The relationship between rulers and ruled grows directly out of production itself and reacts upon it as a determining class e.g. under capitalism the bourgeoisie and the proletariat.
But all that is solid melts into air to quote Marx and that is precisely what happened in firstly February and then decisively in October 1917. To quote the title of John Reed's account it was ten days that shook the world. Thus, it as I have argued was a qualitative change after a series of quantitative changes. The dialectic acted out in history. Ivan Turgenev had illustrated the stirrings, the early quantitative murmurings. Followed by the qualitative change of the revolution debated between Serge and Trotsky and finally Miéville being generically derailed by the defeat and its wake. Following Lukacs I argued for variants on Realist literature and understood

I also suggested that the inability of German philosophy especially Kant to solve the 'subject-object' problem created the potential for a remedy appearing in Hegelian dialectics and Lukacs solving the world-historic problem in 'the identical-subject- object' of the proletariat in communism. Here I argued, following Trotsky, the immense creative potential of human labour would be 'sublimated' into art and literature. This is because for Marx what differentiates humans from other species is imagination as here in Capital Volume One:

We presuppose labour in a form that stamps it as exclusively human. A spider conducts operations that resemble those of a weaver, and a bee puts to shame many an architect in the construction of her cells. But what distinguishes the worst architect from the best of bees is this, that the architect raises his structure in imagination before he erects it in reality. At the end of every labour-process, we get a result that already existed in the imagination of the labourer at its commencement. .

My dissertation will now finally examine a recent and, I will argue, substantial contribution to Marxist aesthetics by the late John Molyneux in his last text The Dialectics of Art published in 2020. Molyneux found inspiration in Trotsky's theory of art and literature. He first 'wrote an analysis of his theory of revolution in 1983. But his theories on Literature and Art made a huge impression.' Molyneux continues:

But by far the most significant theoretical influences on my ideas about art have been Marx and Engels themselves. Marx's theory of alienation and alienated labour, first expounded in the Economic and Philosophic Manuscripts of 1844 (which I read in 1968) and then developed through the Grundrisse and on into Capital, has been a continual point of return and provides the foundation for my answer to the 'What is art?' Equally important is the Marxist theory of history, historical materialism. I am a convinced historical materialist and approach the French Revolution or, indeed, contemporary politics. In relation to art, it is crucial that the historical materialism we are talking about is not any kind of crude or mechanical economic determinism.... In relation to art, it is necessary to remember that art both arises out of (and is always conditioned by) a definite historical and social context – a concrete moment.

In a manner reminiscent of my position Molyneux also references Engels late letters. He continues to suggest, correctly in my view, 'it is evident that all works of art – symphonies and poems and dances and songs and films, as well as paintings and sculptures – have in common the fact that they are all produced by human labour, mental and physical.'5. He is in the tradition of scientific Marxism arguing from Engel's The Part Played by Labour in the Transition from Ape to Man; 'the entire so
- called history of the world is nothing but the begetting of man through human labour.'

John then makes a pertinent point, writers are not compelled to put pen to paper in the same way a 'wage-slave' is blighted to sell their labour, Thus artistic production is unalienated labour. However, Molyneux concedes that other forms of labour are unalienated i.e. political agitation. However, when unalienated labour is structured with both artistic form and content this is another form of labour; unalienated artistic labour. John quotes Marx on Milton in support. Nevertheless, he insists on a contrast between writing simply for a wage, for money, as a mere means to earn a living, and writing as an end in itself.
Milton, for example, who wrote Paradise Lost, was an unproductive worker. In contrast to this, the writer who delivers hackwork for his publisher is a productive worker. Milton produced Paradise Lost in the way that a silkworm produces silk, as the expression of his own nature. Later on, he sold the product for £ 5 and to that extent became a dealer in a commodity. But the Leipzig literary proletarian who produces books, e.g. compendia on political economy, at the instructions of his publisher is roughly speaking a productive worker, in so far as his production is subsumed

under capital and only takes place for the purpose of the latter's vaporization.

Like him I maintain the conditions for a universalized and socialized aesthetic can only occur in the highest stage of human development: communism.
Molyneux concludes:

[...] art is work produced by unalienated human labour and characterised by a fusion or unity of form and content. Furthermore, there is a connection between these two elements in the definition in that, generally speaking, it requires unalienated labour to achieve such a fusion of form and content.
Support from the Marxist Tradition. To the best of my knowledge, the precise definition of art presented here has not been advanced previously.

I suggest John Molyneux's conceptualization of literature and. art provides the potential for further research into the area of Marxist aesthetics for other scholars.

Chapter One Bibliography.
Primary Sources.
China Melville Home - Salvage (accessed 03/12/2023).
China Melville, The City and The City (London, Pan Books, 2009).
 Victor Serge Conquered City (London, Victor Gollancz Ltd, 1976).
Ivan Turgenev Fathers and Sons (trans) Richard Freeborn (Oxford, Oxford University Press, Oxford World Classics, 1998).

Secondary Sources.
Aristotle Poetics The Internet Classics Archive | Poetics by Aristotle
Theodor W. Adorno Aesthetic Theory, (London, Bloomsbury Academic, 2023).
 Ernst Bloch, Atheism in Christianity (New York, Herder, and Herder, 1972).
Ernst Bloch, On Karl Marx (London, Verso, 2018).
Augusto Boal, Theatre of the Oppressed, (London, Pluto Press; 2019).
Steven Cahn, M.; Ross, Stephanie; Shapshay, Sandra L. Aesthetics: A
Comprehensive Anthology (Blackwell Philosophy Anthologies) Wiley. Kindle Edition.
 Howard Cargill, 'Walter Benjamin's Concept of Cultural History,' in The Cambridge Companion to Walter Benjamin, ed. by David S. Ferris, Cambridge Companions to Literature (Cambridge: Cambridge University Press, 2004), pp. 73–96
Tony Cliff, State Capitalism in Russia (London, Bookmarks, 2022).
Neil Davidson, Realism, Modernism, and the Spectre of Trotsky, Part 1: Lukács
Red Wedge, Issue 3, 2017.
Terry Eagleton, The Real Thing Reflections on a Literary Form (London, Yale University Press, 2024).
T.S. Eliot Tradition and Individual Talent in Selected Essays of T. S. Eliot (London, Faber & Faber, 1975

Pual Samiran Kumar. Literary Theory and Marxist Criticism Notion Press. Kindle Edition.

Georg Lukacs, History and class consciousness: studies in Marxist dialectics Accessed 07/12/2023.

Georg Lukacs Lenin: a study in the unity of his thought. (London, New Left Books, 1977).

Georg Lukacs The Destruction of Reason (London, Verso, 2021).

Georg Lukacs, The Meaning of Contemporary Realism, 07/12/2023.

Georg Lukacs The Theory of the Novel (1971) Kindle version.

Karl Marx (1844) Private Property and Communism.

Karl Marx & Frederick Engels Selected Correspondence, (Moscow, Progress Publishers, 1975).

Frederick Engels, https://www.marxists.org/archive/marx/works/1888/letters/88_04_15.htm

Karl Marx and Frederick Engels, The German Ideology, in Collected Works, vol. 5
(New York: International Publishers, 1976).

Marx and Engels Through the Eyes of Their Contemporaries, (Moscow, Progress Publisher, 1972).

'Revelling in Genre: An Interview with China Miéville."

John Molyneux The Dialectics of Art (Chicago, Haymarket Books, 2020).

Salvage magazine. Home - Salvage

Stefan Morawski & Daly Macdonald. Karl Marx and Frederick Engels on Literature and Art, Critical, Cultural and Communications Press. Kindle Edition.

Alan Singer & Allen Dunn, Literary Aesthetics a reader. (Oxford, Blackwell Publishers Ltd, 2001).

Leon Trotsky, Leon Trotsky: Class and Art (1924) - Marxists Internet Archive. Accessed 08/12/2023.

Leon Trotsky, Literature and Revolution, https://www.marxists.org/archive/trotsky/1924/lit_revo/index.htm Accessed 08/12/2023.

Leon Trotsky The Revolution Betrayed (New York, Pathfinder, 1973).

Ivan Turgenev, Literary Reminiscences: And
Autobiographical Fragments (Chicago,
Ivan R Dee, 2001).
Adolfo Sanchez Vazquez, Art, and Society. Essays in
Marxist Aesthetics (London, Merlin Press, 1979).
Susan Weismann, Victor Serge: A Political Biography
(London, Verso, 2013).

Chapter Two.
Primary Sources.

Ivan Turgenev, Fathers and Sons trans. Richard Freeborn (Oxford, Oxford World's Classics).
Ivan Turgenev Hamlet and Don Quixote trans. Robert Nichols (London, Henderson's, 1930).

Secondary Sources
.

Frederick Engels Letter to Margret Hargest. Letters: Marx-Engels Correspondence 1888 - Marxists Internet Archive
Frederick Engels Franz Mehring: On Historical Materialism (Engels' Letter)
Barbara Foley Marxist Literary Criticism Today (London, Pluto Press, 2019).
Richard Freeborn, The Russian Revolutionary Novel: Turgenev to Pasternak, (Cambridge, Cambridge University Press, 1982).
Richard Freeborn, Turgenev: the novelist's novelist, a study. (Oxford, Oxford University Press, 1960).
Emma Goldman, "Intellectual Proletarians "Mother Earth 8, no. 12 (February 1914) "Intellectual Proletarians" Intellectual Proletarians | The Anarchist Library
Frederic Jameson, Marxism and Form: 20th-Century Dialectical Theories of Literature (Princeton, Princeton University Press,1974)
A. V. Knowles, Ivan Turgenev (Boston, Massachusetts, Twayne Publishers, 1988).
V.I. Lenin On Literature and Art (Moscow, Progress Publishers, 1978).
V.I. Lenin, The Three Sources and Three Component Parts of Marxism (1913).
Georg Lukács, The Theory of the Novel (1971 Kindle edition).
Georgi Lukács Writer and Critic (London, Merlin Press, 1978).
Karl Marx & Frederick Engels On Literature and Art (Moscow, Progress Publishers,1976).

Karl Marx and Frederick Engels Selected Correspondence, (Moscow, Progress Publishers, 1955).
Karl Marx and Frederick Engels Selected Works in Three Volumes (Moscow, Progress Publishers, 1973).
Karl Marx & Frederick Engels, January 21, 1882, London. https://www.marxists.org/archive/marx/works/1848/communi st- manifesto/preface.htm#preface-1882
S.S. Prawer Marxism and World Literature (Oxford, Clarendon Press, 1976).
Irina N. Sizemskya, 'Russian Studies in Philosophy, vol. 56, no. 5, 2018.'
Leon Trotsky Leon Trotsky on Literature and Art (New York, Pathfinder,1970).
Leon Trotsky: Literature and Revolution (4. Futurism).

Chapter Three.
Primary Sources.

Victor Serge, Birth of our Power Birth of Our Power: Serge, Victor: Free Download, Borrow, and ...

Victor Serge Conquered City, trans Richard German (London, Victor Gollancz, 1976).

Victor Serge Men in Prison. Serge, Victor, 1890-1947 - Archive.org

Victor Serge. Notebooks: 1936-1947 (New York Review Books Classics). New York Review Books. Kindle Edition.2019).

Victor Serge, Revolution in Danger: Writings from Russia, 1919-1921 (Translated & edited by Ian Birchall), (London, Redwords, 1997).

Victor Serge, Russia Twenty Years After trans. Max Schachman (New York, Pioneer Publishers, 1937).

Secondary sources.

Tony Cliff, Trotsky Vol 3 Fighting the Rising Stalinist Bureaucracy 1923–1927. Tony Cliff - Marxists Internet Archive
Tony Cliff State Capitalism in Russia (London, Bookmarks, 2022).
David Cotterill, The Serge Trotsky Papers: Correspondence and Other Writings Between Victor Serge and Leon Trotsky. (London, Pluto Press, 1994). Kindle Ed.
Frederick Engels Letter to Mehring Franz Mehring: On Historical Materialism (Engels' Letter)
Karl Marx & Frederick Engels On Literature and Art (Moscow, Progress Publishers,1976).
Karl Marx & Frederick Engels Selected Correspondence, (Moscow, Progress Publishers, 1975).

Karl Marx and Frederick Engels Selected Works in Three Volumes (Moscow, Progress Publishers, 1973).
From Revolutionary History, Vol. 5 No. 3, Autumn 1994, pp. 260–2. Transcribed by Alun
Morgan for the Revolutionary History Website.
Marked up by Etinde for the Encyclopaedia of Trotskyism On-Line (ETOL)
Leon Trotsky, History of the Russian Revolution. First published 1932 Published in Penguin Classics 2017 Copyright © 1932 Max Eastman, renewed 1961 (now held by Yvette Eastman) (Penguin Modern Classics) Penguin Books Ltd. Kindle Edition.
Leon Trotsky The Revolution Betrayed (London, Pathfinder, 2001).
Soviet Writers' Congress 1934 (London, Lawrence, and Wishart, 1977).
Alan Woods and Ted Grant, Lenin, and Trotsky – What they really stood for. Wellred Books.

Chapter Four.

Theodor Adorno, Noten Zur Literature. (1973).Noten Zur Literatur / 2 : Adorno, Theodor W - Archive.org
Ernst Bloch. (1976).Atheism in Christianity : the religion of the Exodus and the Kingdom ...

Ernst Bloch, Ernst Bloch, Geist der Utopia, (The Spirit of Utopia), translated by Anthony A. Nassar, Stanford University Press, Stanford, 2000).

Alexander Bogdanov Red Star trans. Charles Rouge (USA Indiana University Press, 1984).

Terry Eagleton, Marxism and Literary Criticism. Taylor and Francis. Kindle Edition.

Carl Freedman, Art, and Idea in the Novels of China Miéville (SF Story worlds: Critical Studies
in Science Fiction Book 3). Gylphi Lim

Gareth Jenkins, "Book Review", Socialist Review, September
2009,
http://www.socialistreview.org.uk/article.php?articlenumber=10942 Archived 1 7 February 2013 at the Wayback Machine

V.I Lenin, Collected Works 31, (Moscow/London, 1966),

Georg Lukács The Meaning of Contemporary Realism, trans. by John and Necke Mander (London: Merlin Press, 1979).

Marx, Karl; Engels, Friedrich; Lenin, V.I.; Trotsky, Leon; Plekhanov, George; Luxemburg, Rosa. Edited by John Peterson Introduction by Alan Woods The Revolutionary Philosophy of Marxism: Selected Writings on Dialectical Materialism. Wellred Books.2018.

Mathew Sangster, An Introduction to Fantasy (Cambridge: Cambridge University Press, 2023),

Leon Trotsky, Writings On Literature And Art: And Literature And Revolution. (New York, Pathfinder.1972) Kindle Edition.

Alan Woods The History of Philosophy: A Marxist Perspective UK distribution: Wellred Books, wellredbooks.net
London, books@wellredbooks.net 2021

Conclusion.

Frederick Engels The Part Played by Labour in the Transition from Ape to Man.
The Part Played by Labor in the Transition From Ape to Man

V.I. Lenin. The State and Revolution the state and revolution: V. I. Lenin : Free Download, Borrow, and ...
Karl Marx, Capital, vol. I (1867). Online at https://www.marxists.org/archive/marx/works/1867-c1/ch07.htm
Karl Marx, Capital, Vol. III (New York: International Publishers, 1967), p. 791.
Karl Marx, Theories of Surplus Value (Moscow, Progress Publishers, 1963)
Karl Marx and Frederick Engels, The German Ideology (New York: International Publishers, 1947),

John Molyneux The Dialectics of Art (Chicago, Haymarket, 2020)

Upon reading Victor Serge's novel Conquered City.
An English Sonnet on an early scheme of Thomas Wyatt.

Serge's novel was written under the conditions of the Stalinist counter- revolution in 1932 and paints a challenging picture of 'War Communism' 1919-21 in Petrograd. A time of love & hate, hope & despair, and the Red Terror. The octave delineates the circumstances of Petrograd, White (counter-revolutionary) spies, traitors as well as the Bolsheviks desperately hanging on. This is answered in the sestet which suggests the Red Terror as described by Victor Serge. The Red Army and many of the citizens of Petrograd were victorious but at a high price. Rydin declares at the end of the novel: 'It was necessary. It was necessary.'
Rhyme scheme: ABBAABBA CDDC EE The octave presents the argument which is answered by the sestet.

> They seem to be so dry that mate,
> But take the line without our thirst,
> They do not forge plans in the mist,
> But begin to talk on obscured tape.
> We reply using the corrected state,
> Not divulging a thing that is amiss,
> They smile and try to cast some bliss,
> We grimace at their bacon fat Fate.
>
> Red Terror does just crack at dawn,
> We have all of them scribed in red,
> They all will crawl into a piggy bed,
> To talk with those that also do fawn.
> Who are trapped in Tzarina's crown,
> Zombies who grunt, spew and moan.

Fathers and Sons. Notes on Realism in Turgenev literature.
' This analysis argues that although literary 'form' is determined by the socio-economic conditions i.e. form is determined by the content it embodies and as the social 'mode of production' changes the nature of that 'content' is transformed and therefore effects the 'form'(see Eagleton

(1976). That there is not a 'reflex' connection between them and that by examining the way 'form' is used in Fathers and Sons' (1863), in the light of the modern Realist novel developed by Lukcas. We can comprehend how Realist and non-Realist techniques achieve a 'totality'. I shall argue that Marx (1859) constructs a persuasive theoretical model which can be applied to the Realist Novel. However this must be understood in the context of a 'dialectical' relationship between 'form' and 'content' Hegel (1831). Having applied Lukcas' model to Turgenev (1863) especially his ideas of 'typicality' (by this he means an individualized character combined with a 'world historic' epoch, 'world historic' can defined as a 'progressive' historical epoch e.g. the period in Russia during 1860's) and I argue that because Bazarov was both a 'typical' and 'world historic' character and therefore the novel achieves a 'totality' i.e. a 'balance of 'general and particular and also the conceptual and sensuous' (Eagleton 1976). Was he prime 'New Man in the Realist Novel? I contest this with reference to Turgenev Hamlet and Quixotic (1860). Consequently we can comprehend the roots of the decline of the Realist Novel into both Naturalism and into Formalism with the concomitant rise of 'irrationalism' Lukcas(1938).I argue that this degeneration originated from the 'idea' of 'the superfluous man' Turgenev (1850) in Russian literature which itself was the product of material conditions. I will illustrate these claims by close reference to the text and in particular contrasting Realist and non-Realist literary techniques. Clear socio-economic forces influenced the 19th century Realist novel a) the convolutions caused in Western Europe would spread West b) the defeat of Imperial Russia in the Crimean War (1853-6) and the rise of the razanochinets new class of educated young men and women who were not aligned with the ruling class and estranged from the 'traditions' and who acted on their beliefs. this concept found its highest manifestation in 'What is to be Done? Chernyshevsky: (1863). Fathers and Sons is composed of both Realist and non-Realist elements. It's not a political trait that is masquerading as a Realist model and confined by the dictates 'socialist Realism as in 'Mother: Gorky (1903) nor is it t an example of 'genre' of another form of distorted Realist form such as 'the Naturalism of Zola in 'Germinal': 'By naturalism Lukcas means the distortion of realism which merely photographs the surface phenomena of society without penetrating to their significant essences.' Eagleton (1976) p 28. Turgenev employs some basic Realist methods, at the beginning of the book we are introduced to an 'Omniscient Narrator who can describe the 'plot' but also, significantly see into the 'essences', the 'totalities' that Lukcas maintains is the central aspect of Realism; If a writer strives to represent reality as it truly is, i.e. if he is an authentic realist, then the question of totality plays ad decisive role. ibid. Turgenev immediately acquaints us with an omniscient narrator i.e. who both describes and sees beyond the surface: 'We will acquaint the reader with him 'His name is Nicolai Petrovich Korsakov. Turgenev (1863) p 1. This is immediately 'counter-balanced' by an account of the Korsakov's own account of his life as both social history in which we are given unique access to his character not as the product dialogue but all-seeing narrator; portentously we are told:: but then along came 1848' ibid p. 5. The year which revolutions swept Europe. Soon this ere is a connecting passage of 'dialogue' which also has the quality of 'showing' 'Dad let me introduce my good friend Bazarov....' 'Sincerely glad, 'h began, and grateful to you for kindly intending to stay with us…Permit me to ask your name…' 'Evegeny Vasilev' Bazarov answered in a lazy but manly voice.' ibid p.7. This is an example of both Turgenev's ability to combine Realist technique and aspects of his 'style' in this dialogue, it is an apparently straightforward piece of Realism but an 'atmosphere' is being created: 'As a conjurer of atmosphere Turgenev had no equal.' Freeborn (2001). p. 105. I would argue that 'atmosphere is similar to 'essence'; Turgenev has looked beyond the objective 'material reality' in a fashion 'typical' of Realist technique, indeed here is employing a technique used by Austin of 'polarized characters' e.g. Elizabeth and Mrs Bennett. However I would suggest that Turgenev's characters to do possess that opposition of and 'roundness' and 'flatness respectively found in the Austin's two mentioned. They are character in a seminal example of the Realist genre in Pride and Prejudice Austin (1818). But in the 19th century Realist novel, the characters and in particular Bazarov transcend this. They develop in the context of their societal circumstances i.e. in the 'content' but the unique 'form' then rebounds to transform the 'content' which, in turn affects the socio-economic conditions from which it has arisen. While juxtaposing Austin and Turgenev it is of interest to examine Freeborn a comment made by Freeborn regarding Turgenev: 'he succeeded in creating the world of the ... country estate so perfectly that no other writer has surpassed him.' Freeborn (2001) This is significant in several ways, firstly Freeborn is suggesting the great technical skill in 'showing' and 'telling' to produce the 'totality' of the country estate and secondly the importance of this 'setting' in Turgenev (1863) because of the physical limitations he imposed the characters are is using the technique of 'concentration' in which he characters emotions are intensified and they experience a number of realizations. An example of this is Chapter 17; Odintosva is talking about her life with Bazarov in her 'country estate'. was firstly provided with an example 'telling' by the narrator, this is a fundamental Realist Technique: 'The estate where Anna Sergeevna lived stood on a bare sloping hill a short distance from a yellow stone church with a green roof and white pillars' Turgenev (1883) p 81. I shall attempt to illustrate firstly the complex relationship between 'content' and 'form' 'The work of the German left-wing Hegelian whose Essence of Christianity (1841) had a major impact in Russia in the 1840's embraced a materialist outlook.' Oxford (2009) p129 Hence the 'social context of Turgenev (1883) influence its 'content' which acted the 'form' and its automatons development: 'Art possess a high degree of autonomy.' Trotsky (1924) Baranov's crude Materialism emanates from Feuerbach (1841): He addresses Odintosva: 'You're healthy, independent and wealthy-what more could you want?'' 'What do I want…yes, I'm old…and ahead of me a long, long road with nothing to aim for…I just don't want to go down it.' 'You're disillusioned.' Turgenev (1883) p. 97/8.

Two main aspects of Turgenev's technique are illustrated here 1) the use of dialogue as a means to create characterization but 2) this is an epiphany for both characters a) Baranov begins to see the constraints of pre-Marxist Materialism, b) Odintosva experiences an 'existential crisis' and they both realize they share an estrangement from Russian society and, indeed, the natural world. We can understand how on page 81+97/8 Turgenev uses the 'conjuncture' of 'telling' followed by 'dialogue' to create this moment of realization. The main emphasis of 'focalization' in Fathers and Sons is on Baranov because he is 'the centre of consciousnesses of the narrative. Bazarov is an example of Turgenev's complex characterization a): he a fictional figure and b) a figure based on a young doctor Turgenev had met and c) a 'typical' character. In 'Studies in European Realism (1972) and The Historical Novel (1962) Lukcas explained his ideas on the Realist novel. As I have illustrated Bazarov embodied what Lukcas called 'typical' character which must live in a 'World Historic' epoch' without being submerged in them and is therefore 'individualized. I would argue that the 1860's as such a period. For Lukcas what created a great realist novelist was not individual ability but: 'the richness and profundity of created characters relies upon the richness and profundity of the social process.' New Hungarian Quarterly (Autumn 1972) Finally, Turgenev although a great Realist writer derived much from non-realist sources and applied then in his novels. In Hamlet and Don Queitite (1860) they are seen as opposite poles; one introspective, the other lives outside of his psyche and is capable of self-sacrifice This is an non-realist model constructed above, and shows Turgenev' flaw, his 'superfluous man' (1850) who has radical words but no action can be seen in Bazarov while the prototype for the Bolsheviks would be Chernyshevsky (1863) heroine Vera Pavlovna. Turgenev was not: 'On the threshold of the future' Turgenev: (Oxford 2001) p 132. We can comprehend the roots of the decline of the Realist Novel into both Naturalism Lukcas (1938) an originating in the non-Realist' of 'the superfluous man' Turgenev (1850).

Bibliography

Austin, J Pride and Prejudice (1813) Oxford World Classics.

Chernyshevsky (1863) in ed Cornwael I Routledge Guide to Russian Literature Routledge.

Eagleton, T (1989) Marxism and Literary Criticism Routledge.

Freeborn The Classic Russian Novel in Cornwell, I ed The Routledge guide to Russian Literature. Routledge

Hegel, F. (1831) Philosophy of Fine Art in Eagleton (1989) Marxism and literary Criticism Routledge

Lukcas. (1971) The Theory of the Novel London in Eagleton, T (1989) Marxism and literary Criticism Routledge.

Marx, K, (1977) Selected Works OUP. New Hungarian Quarterly Autumn 1972.

Oxford Nineteenth Century Thought and Literature in Cornwell, I ed The Routledge Guide to Russian Literature Routledge.

John Milton Paradise Lost.

How Cruel is the Story of Eve – Stevie Smith.
How cruel is the story of Eve
What responsibility
It has in history.
For cruelty.
Touch, where the feeling is most vulnerable
Unblameworthy - ah reckless - desiring children,
Touch there with a touch of pain?
Abominable.
Ah what cruelty,
In history.
What misery.
Put up to barter,
The tender feelings
Buy her a husband to rule her
Fool her to marry a master
She must or rue it
The Lord said it.
And man, poor man,
Is he fit to rule,
Pushed to it?
How can he carry it, the governance,
And not suffer for it
Insuffisance?
He must make woman lower then
So he can be higher then.
Oh what cruelty,
In history, what misery.
Soon woman grows cunning,
Masks her wisdom,
How otherwise will he
Brnig food and shelter, kill enemies?
If he did not feel superior
It would be the worse for her
And for the tender children
Worse for them.
Oh what cruelty,

In history what misery
Of falsity.
It is only a legend,
You say? But what
Is the meaning of the legend
If not
To give blame to women most
And most punishment?
This is the meaning of a legend that colours
All human thought; it is not found among animals.
How cruel is the story of Eve,
What responsibility it has
In history
For misery.
Yet there is this to be said still,
Life would be over long ago
If men and women had not loved each other
Naturally, naturally,
Forgetting their mythology,
They would have died of it else
Long ago, long ago,
And all would be emptiness now
And silence.
Oh dread Nature, for your purpose,
To have made them love so.
 (from Poems, 1962, 1966)
She was a great poet. Rejecting the Anglican Communion,
controversially, in 1961 over the Question of Evil.
Specifically, how could an omniscient and omnibenevolent
Divinity

 Plekhanov commented:
'The social mentality of an age is conditioned by its social
conditions this is nowhere quite as evident as in the history
of art and literature.'

(Eagleton 1976, p. 6),

The value of art to the artist then is this, that it makes him free. It appears to him of value as a self-expression, but in fact it is not the expression of a self but the discovery of a self. It is the creation of a self. In synthesising his experience with society's, in pressing his inner self into the mould of social relations, he not only creates a new mould, a socially valuable product, but he also moulds and creates his own self. The mute inglorious Milton is a fallacy. Miltons are made, not born.

-         Christopher Caudwell, Culture and Politics, Selected Work p. 10.

In The Political Unconscious, Fredric Jameson formulates the relations of text, interpretive tradition and totalizing Marxist analysis in a way that gives point to my present concerns. Jameson points out that "we never really confront a text immediately, in all its freshness as a thing-in-itself." On the contrary, texts are grasped "through the sedimented layers of previous interpretations" or, in the case of a new text, "through the sedimented reading habits and categories developed by those interpretive traditions."

The Fruits of One's Labor in Miltonic Practice and Marxian Theory
Marshall Grossman
ELH, Vol. 59, No. 1 (Spring, 1992), pp. 77-105 (29 pages)
https://doi.org/10.2307/2873419•https://www.jstor.org/stable/2873419

Milton, for example, who did Paradise Lost, was an unproductive worker. In contrast to this, the writer who delivers hackwork for his publisher is a productive worker. Milton produced Paradise Lost in the way that a silkworm produces silk, as the expression of his own nature. Later on he sold the product for £5 and to that extent became a dealer in a commodity.'

                              - Karl Marx. Theories of Surplus Value, Part I (Moscow, n.d.), p. 389

See below: Christopher Caudwell, Politics as Culture, Selected Writings, p. 130-32.

Extracts from a paper on aesthetics where I rely on the work of John Molyneux:
The fact that art is non-alienated labour cannot
be the end of the story because there is a great
deal of unalienated labour that is not and does not
produce art.
- Molyneux, John. (2020) The Dialectics of Arts. P, 38. Haymarket Books. Kindle Edition.

So how can we define when unalienated labour is art and when it is not? Molyneux provided an explanation:
The answer lies in the nature of the relationship between
form and content that prevails in these categories, as
opposed to the relationship that obtains in art. In a work of
scientific or social theory, the content is not only much more
important than the form,
but it is also, to a large extent, detachable from it. In a work
of art the content/meaning is totally bound up with the form
and is inseparable from it.... And by 'form', I do not mean
genre or formal structure, as in a poem that is a sonnet or in
rhyming couplets, or in a watercolour painting, or in music, a
blues piece, or a concerto. I mean the concrete form of a
particular work: in the case of a poem, every single word in
that exact order.
- Molyneux, John (2020) p. 39. Haymarket Books. Kindle Edition.
John Molyneux concluded his position with a sense of satisfaction, which is appropriate in my opinion because this is an advance in Marxian, indeed all aesthetics:
To conclude, art is work produced by unalienated human labour and characterised by a fusion or unity of form and content. Furthermore, there is a connection between these two elements in the definition in that, generally speaking, it requires unalienated labour to achieve such

a fusion of form and content.... To the best of my knowledge, the precise definition of art presented here has not been advanced previously,

- Molyneux, John (2020) p. 42.
Haymarket Books. Kindle Edition.

 Yet the theologians were themselves keenly aware of such contradictions, which were registered virtually from the beginnings of Christian theory in the problem of whether God himself can be said to have willed evil. Milton seems to have solved this problem to his own intellectual satisfaction in a disarming way: by separating God's will from God's foreknowledge. Knowing how a thing is going to turn out is quite a different matter from wanting it to turn out that way; God knows in advance what Adam will decide, what Eve will do, but that does not mean he likes it, nor does it mean that they were not free to do otherwise. Three observations need to be made about this solution, and the first has to do with the relations between freedom, temporal perspective and explanation.

We do not seem to have any great difficulty in reconciling the two temporal perspectives on an act: the freedom of choice that precedes it, and the possibility of explanation that now weighs the completed act (including the reasons and the freedom of choice that went into its execution). Yet perhaps that is only because we do not pose the problem sharply enough, to the point where it becomes revealed as an antimony, as an unthinkable paradox or aporia. Consider, for instance, Gide's little fable, Lafcadio's Adventures, which is about a man exasperated by the humiliation of having his acts judged and explained, most immediately by the behaviourists and the positivists, who see everything you do as being determined, but more generally in any kind of character judgement, in which other people say, Well of course he would have done that: he's that kind of person (spiteful, generous, indecisive, etc. - all judgements which reify you by making your character into a kind of determinism in its own right). So Lafcadio, in order to evade this reifying judgement and to remain free, invents a new kind of ethics, that of the famous gratuitous act or acte gratuit, the act that absolutely evades all ex post facto explanation. In the final irony of the novel, a stray button provides evidence that the murder which Lafcadio designed to embody this absolute gratuitousness is on the contrary susceptible of the most banal explanation and motivation possible, namely that of simple jealousy. Meanwhile, in the later Sartrean versions of this dilemma, the screw is given yet another turn by a final reifying judgement by other people: if such and such does this gratuitous and absolutely unmotivated thing, then the reason is obvious: it is to keep us guessing; in fact, it is quite in character and quite motivated, since the person in question is very precisely defined as capricious. These ethical fables serve to suggest that there may be something absolutely incommensurable between the temporal perspective of action, the choice and the project; and that of explanation, of meaning, of inevitability. My other two observations will be briefer: on the one hand, it is clear that even Milton's category of foreknowledge still presupposes the organizational framework of an individual subject. We will return to this point in a moment. And the other point is related to this one, but is too complex for me to develop here at any length: it is this, that the ethical categories, the ethical binaries of good and evil, to which the Providential vision is irredeemably shackled, are to my mind the ultimate form of ideological closure, far more damaging and influential in the long run than either metaphysics or idealism, which have traditionally been the ways in which ideological false consciousness has been characterized. Nietzsche taught us, however, not merely that ethics is absolutely a projection of the positioning of the individual subject (what's good is what's related to my self, to the centre; what's evil is what is other, eccentric, marginalized), but also that all genuine historical and political thought must somehow do the impossible and invent an intellectual space for itself 'beyond good and evil', that is to say, beyond the categories of ethics. Now I will say that, with these qualifications, the idea of Providence is the distorted anticipation, within the religious and figural master-code, of the idea of historical necessity in historical materialism. Yet this idea is fully as widely misconstrued and misunderstood as the other, and demands some explanation in its own right. The doctrine of historical inevitability is not, as Popper thought, a 'belief of any kind, and certainly not a belief in the predictability of future events: to put it another way, it is not a teleology and has nothing to do with an eschatological certainty about the end of history. The function of this concept is a far more disappointingly modest and descriptive one, which we may characterize by saying the notion of historical inevitability or historical necessity is simply the enabling presupposition of the historian herself, and governs the form with which historiography endows the events of the past, the things that have already happened once and for all. The concept of historical necessity is simply the assumption that things happened the way they did because they had to happen that way and no other, and that the business of the historian is to show why they had to happen that way. If you like, then, this is a pseudo-idea: it could have real meaning only if you were able somehow to repeat the past or replay the tape under controlled experimental or laboratory conditions.... But the Calvinist and the Leninist solutions to these dilemmas are perfectly sensible, provided you understand how profoundly Hegelian both of them are. For Hegel's is the only consequent way of formulating the problem, and for better or for worse we have got no further than his slogan: the owl of Minerva flies at dusk, historical necessity is visible only after the fact, the historical understanding - what Hegel calls Absolute Spirit - is only called into play on the Sunday of life, after action and praxis are over, when history for however brief a moment has come to a stop. Hegel's 'solution' is thus a thoroughgoing double standard, in which the past is necessary and its chain of events as inevitable as in any Providential scheme, but where this understanding of necessity has nothing whatsoever to do with the possibilities of action in the present. The Kairos is then Lenin in April: you cannot know whether a thing was possible until it is tried; only after the fact does it transpire that what finally happened had to happen that way and no other. All of which - these anticipatory relationships between Marxism's notion of historical inevitability and providential religion - may be taken as a gloss and commentary on Walter Benjamin's enigmatic opening image, in the Theses on the Philosophy of History, of the chess-playing automaton with the dwarf hidden inside it to guide its moves: 'The puppet called "historical materialism" is to win all the time. It can easily be a match for anyone if it enlists the services of theology, which today, as we know, is wizened and has to keep out of sight' (Benjamin 1968, p. 253). The paradox here evidently turns on the sense of the expression 'to win'. Meanwhile, the Hegelian and retrospective character of historical knowledge is underscored in another image from this same text, perhaps the most famous of all, on Klee's Angelus Novus: His face is turned toward the past. Where we perceive a chain of events, he sees one single catastrophe which keeps piling wreckage upon wreckage and hurls it in front of his feet. The angel would like to say, awaken the dead, and make whole what has been smashed. But a storm is blowing from Paradise; it has caught in his wings with such violence that the angel can no longer close them. This storm irresistibly propels him into the future to which his back is turned, while the pile of debris before him grows skyward. This storm is what we call progress. (Benjamin 1968, pp. 257-8) Such an image may serve to demonstrate a final proposition about the Hegelian/Marxist notion of historical inevitability which is perhaps less widely understood than anything else; namely that it is not a teleology (unless one could conceive of a teleology after the fact). Nobody today surely believes that anything is inevitable in that teleological sense, certainly not socialism or world revolution. This angel, or Absolute Spirit, cannot look over its shoulder into the future.... onfront the figural mode again, as it were to the second power. Is it possible that this second-degree process of figural articulation - the process of cultural production generally - may do more than simply replicate the flrst; indeed, that it may in some central way serve to foreground and to bring out the contradictions and structural limits of its primary theological raw material? This is at least the theory proposed by Louis Althusser in his Letter on Art and methodologically developed by Pierre Macherey in A Theory of Literary Production: which it will now be useful to test against the case of Milton. The idea is that the act of figuration or representation does not merely illustrate, exemplify or replicate its ideological - we may even say its ideational - content; rather, it decisively transforms the latter, so that what looked initially like an idea or a concept when taken in its purely ideological form (Macherey's central example is Jules Verne's 'idea' of progress) is unmasked as ideology when the artist attempts to give it full representation. The ideological, all the while claiming to project a coherent vision, is always contradictory, always structurally incoherent and ultimately unsusceptible of formal intelligibility. Thus, when ideology is taken at its word and endowed with the beginnings of a visionary, figural or representational form, the impossibility of that representation and the essential incoherence of the ideology itself becomes foregrounded and visible in its own right. This is indeed the very vocation of culture itself for Althusser and Macherey: not to transmit ideology, but rather to make ideology visible as an object, to demystify the ideological, not through conceptual analysis, but through the process of its production as figure and representation. Whatever the absolute value of this theory as a transhistorical description of culture generally, it would certainly seem to have some relevance for a text which explicitly sets out to celebrate, dramatize and justify a preexisting ideology, namely that of Providence... Still, the demands of representation and the epic require Milton to render God anthropomorphically as a character; or, in other words, in our previous terminology, to articulate Providence and the whole theme of foreknowledge of the historical totality within the confines of the individual subject, thus turning history back into a representation offered to that supreme individual consciousness, God; much as, quite against the spirit of his own system, the demands of Hegelian representation end up forcing the latter towards that weaker anthropomorphic personification which is Absolute Spirit.... Parts of De Doctrina document Milton's sense of the way in which anthropomorphic representation distorts and reifies the theologial content of the notions of God and Providence, which we have identified with history; but his Arianism will let us make this point in a more tangible way, and in the process illustrate what was meant earlier by the proposition that such theological issues are not matters of personal 'belief but rather something quite different. In this case, I will suggest that Milton's Arianism - the repudiation of the Trinity and the emphasis on the created, secondary nature of Christ - is less a matter of opinion, heretical or not, but rather first and foremost a result of the requirements and dialectic of figuration. Milton senses that in endowing the place of historical necessity with something like an individual subjectivity, an anthropomorphic appearance, some fundamental ideological incoherence is betrayed: thus, the radical dissociation of the figure of Christ from God, the insistence on Christ's proper status as an actant, a narrative character - as distinct from this other seeming 'character' who is really not one at all, or should not be one becomes an attempt to recontain the contradiction, to limit the ravages of demystification released by the representation process. This reading now allows us to reformulate the positions of William Empson's splendid and passionate book, Milton's God, in a more theoretically adequate way. Leaving aside Empson's admirable eighteenth-century Enlightenment hatred of religion and superstition - which, as I observed initially, is probably not the most productive position for people on the left to take today - what is unsatisfactory about Milton's God is the retention of a framework in which the organizing perspective remains the biographical Milton, as author and individual subject, with his opinions, flaws, weaknesses and strengths, and the like. Surely Empson's detailed account of the tricks and stratagems whereby Milton's God arranges both for Satan and for his human creations to fall, in order to fulfil his original plan; as well as his characterization of the human and sacrificial blood thirstiness of the deity - these things are quite unanswerable: only we would now prefer to take them, less as testimony about Milton's theological beliefs, than as a demonstration of the way in which the requirement to give anthropomorphic figuration to the ideology of Providence ends up denouncing itself, and undermining the very ideology it set out to embody. Yet this is an objective and impersonal, what today would be called a textual, process: by a kind of ruse of reason, Milton's symbolic act is alienated from itself, turns against itself, ends up producing the opposite of what it originally intended. But if this is an accurate description of what happens to ideology in the text, then it may well be a source of embarrassment to the older strategies for political interpretation, whose aim was to enlist the great writer on your side as an individual subject, and to stress the progressive or humanistic characteristics of Shakespeare, Balzac, and most recently of Milton himself, in Christopher Hill's great biography. On the other hand, it must be admitted that the comments we have made so far on Milton's ideology are not yet terribly political either. Perhaps turning our attention from God to Satan will help us make some further progress along these lines. On the face of it, indeed, it would seem a priori quite unavoidable, in the revolutionary situation in which Milton wrote, for Satan's rebellion against God not to give off at least faint overtones of the great Rebellion itself, of the militant revolt against a king by divine right; and this, even if we exclude that other predictable psychological reaction which would involve collective guilt and trauma at that historically unique act which is the public execution of a monarch.

Oddly enough, none of this seems to be present in the text, and the current view of Satan as a great feudal baron seems to stand up well to careful reading: the revolt of a peer has in fact little enough in common with the dynamics of middle-class revolution but a great deal with the convulsions of medieval feudalism or with that anachronistic contemporary event, the Fronde. Thus, the War in Heaven, the prehistory of the Creation before Eden, oddly inscribes a peculiar and anachronistic diachrony within the first great monument of bourgeois literature - a reminiscence of the distant feudal past that would seem to have little enough relevance to the war aims of the New Model Army or the visions of the radical reformation. Still, I think we can locate the place in which the contemporary reference is repressed: and its structural absence, the irritatingly protestant self-righteousness and complacency of that repression, is not unrelated to the figure of Satan, yet in a rather different way than we might have expected. Milton's party need feel no guilt about the revolt against the king for a simple reason, that he is not really a king at all, but something quite different, namely a tyrant: and the latter is defined as himself being a rebel against God's law. Thus, not the regicides, but the king himself is the rebel, occupies the place of Satan: the thrust of the accusation is structurally reversed - I banish you! you are the only guilty party here! But note that the structural displacement achieved by the political unconscious at this crucial point succeeds in eliding something significant: there is henceforth, in this particular narrative apparatus, no longer any place for the army of the saints themselves, for that particular emergent subject of history which is the very protagonist of the bourgeois revolution. There are now two separate strategies for overcoming the tyrant, for triumphing over Satan-Charles, but neither makes a place for a collective actor, and only the first is properly political at all. That is of course secured by God himself before the creation of humankind: and the fall of Satan-Charles - the end of the feudal age - with that archaic reminiscence of feudal warfare on which we have already commented - thus comes before us less as class praxis than as what we might today call a systemic transformation, a break between two modes of production, a virtually structural coupure: one should perhaps summon up a little of E. P. Thompson's indignation with Althusserian structural history in order to deplore this elision of collective praxis and action from the Miltonic narrative...

But when one recalls the more amusing features of the narrative sexism - and in particular the bourgeois interior scene of Books V-VIII where Eve, having served the men, Adam and the angel Raphael, leaves them alone to pursue their scientific discussion, not as not with such discourse

Delighted, or not capable her ear Of what was high: such pleasures she reserved, Adam relating, she sole auditress (VIII, 48-51). the amphetamine-type stimulation of the apple suggests a chance for Eve to speak and to converse with Adam as an equal. At any rate, the marks of Milton's sexism here and throughout are too obvious and too embarrassing (Tor well I understand in the prime end / Of Nature her the inferior', VIII, 540-1) to document at any great length. Meanwhile the poet's courageous defence of divorce has often been celebrated as a progressive position and a contribution to the struggle for social freedom. Is it ungrateful to suggest something Islamic in this conception of a democratic community of males who are free to repudiate their wives? In any case, the limits of Milton's politics - that protestant conservatism and commitment to hierarchy and elite authority which cuts him off from the greater radicalism of his time - is surely profoundly at one with his sexual politics and his belief in the inequality of the sexes. I would only want to resist establishing causal priorities between these two dimensions of the personal and the political, and reconfirming their separation by encouraging the temptation to show that class attitudes condition Milton's sexual politics, or on the other hand that patriarchal values end up programming his public positions in the political field. Yet, as I argued earlier, these personal biases and ideological opinions of the biographical individual John Milton are not really what is at stake here; the point was rather to show that the poem itself inscribes this insight, and faithfully demystifies its own initial raw material (among the latter Milton's private attitudes), designating the latter as ideology and reversing its messages. The official ideological message, the conscious intent of the poem was the defence and justification of the position that sin, the fallen world, the failure of revolutionary politics, all result ultimately from disobedience, from lack of discipline, from insufficient respect for hierarchy. Yet in the second-degree constructivist reading we have proposed this sequence is reversed, and the poetic narrative rather offers testimony of the constitutive relationship between this image of sin and of the fall and the failure to imagine genuine human equality. Eve has to fall, not because she is sinful or disobedient, but because Milton cannot find it in himself to imagine and to give figuration to an equality between the sexes that would open up into a concrete vision of the community of free people. The poem thus illustrates and documents, not a proposition about human nature, not a type of philosophical or theological content, but rather the operation of ideological closure: in this way, a poem in which, as we have said, the political is repressed none the less ends up producing a political reading of itself.

- Fredrick Jameson (2016)Religion and ideology: a political reading of Paradise Lost.

'The Adam and Eve who walk out of Paradise Lost hand in hand are human, practical, down-to-earthy, in a way that might not have been conceivable before Milton's experience in the English Revolution.'

- Hill, Christopher. Milton and the English Revolution.

Christopher Hill discussing Milton's Paradise Lost:
'Raphael's account of the War in Heaven offers many analogies with the English Civil War.
What if earth Be but the shadow of heaven and things therein
Each to other like, more than on earth is thought? (V. 574–6)
Both the heavenly choir ('this new-made world, another heaven' – VII. 617) and Satan confirm ('O earth, how like to heaven' – IX. 99). It was an analogy which Milton had drawn as early as 1641.'
- Hill, Christopher. Milton and the English Revolution. Verso. Kindle Edition.

It is a new barbarism to suppose that an appreciator of an artwork is professionally unconscious of its social background.'
Empson (1961), p. 275

- Hill, Christopher. Milton and the English Revolution. Verso. Kindle Edition.
First, to what extent did Milton diverge from orthodox perceptions of Genesis. Second, how did his own experiences, feelings, allegiances, prejudices and disappointments, play some part in the writing of the poem and, in respect of this, in what ways does it reflect the theological and political tensions of the seventeenth century?
 John Milton (2001). Richard Bradford, p, 94
(Before his visit to Italy Milton had become intimately familiar with the works of Dante Alighieri (1265–1321) whose Divine Comedy was the only major Christian epic prior to Paradise Lost.)
Bradford, (2001) p 23.
The trial and the execution of Charles I drew Milton back into the maelstrom of English political and religious debate. Two weeks after Charles was beheaded Milton published, in February 1649, a pamphlet called The Tenure of Kings and Magistrates, which was and has remained a controversial document. It was written during the trial of the king, the progress and details of which Milton is thought to have been aware; and, with only indirect reference to these events, he investigates their premises and contexts. His thesis is that monarchy holds power by virtue of a tacit contract with the people. If the former fails in this stewardship – and Milton suggests rather than explicitly claims that Charles had done so – it should be called to account by its subjects.
Bradford, Richard. John Milton (Routledge Guides to Literature) (pp. 36-37). Taylor and Francis. Kindle Edition.

Mary Wollstonecraft's Vindication of the Rights of Women (1792) summarises Milton's Eve in these scathing terms: ... when [Milton] tells us that women are formed for softness and sweet attractive grace, I cannot comprehend his meaning, unless, in the true Mahometan strain, he meant to deprive us of souls, and insinuate that we were beings only designed by sweet attractive grace, and docile blind obedience, to gratify the senses of man when he can no longer soar on the wing of contemplation.16
Edwards, M (2015) p, 210.
The conclusion of Virginia Woolf's: A Room of One's Own, 'if we look past Milton's Bogey ... then [the] dead poet who was Shakespeare's sister will put on the body which she has so often laid down'.

'The perfunctory reference to Milton is curiously enigmatic, for the allusion has had no significant development, and Woolf, in the midst of her peroration, does not stop to explain it. Yet the context in which she places this apparently mysterious bogey is highly suggestive. Shutting out the view, Milton's bogey cuts women off from the spaciousness of possibility, the predominantly male landscapes of fulfilment Woolf has been describing throughout A Room. Worse, locking women into "the common sitting room" that denies them individuality, it is a murderous phantom that, if it didn't actually kill "Judith Shakespeare," has helped to keep her dead for hundreds of years, over and over again separating her creative spirit from "the body which she has so often laid down."
Gilbert, Sandra M.; Gubar, Susan. The Madwoman in the Attic (Veritas Paperbacks) (p. 188). Yale University Press. Kindle Edition.

- 		Seeds of disobedience: Milton's early descriptions of Eve.
Sandra M. Gilbert, feminist perspective.
From the start, however, the poet emphasises the hierarchical distinction between Adam and Eve, the

primordial pair. As Satan, journeying to Eden bent on revenge against God, first views them, Adam and Eve are:
Not equal, as their sex not equal seem'd;
For contemplation hee and valour form'd,
For softness shee and sweet attractive Grace,
Hee for God only, shee for God in him;
His fair large Front and Eye sublime declar'd
Absolute rule ... (Book 4, ll. 294–99)
… while Eve, with hair 'Dishhevell'd ... in wanton ringlets' (Book 4, l. 304), appears an image of 'coy submission, modest pride' (Book 4, l. 308). With her lower status, dishevelled hair and wanton ringlets, the reader is prepared by the poet, quite early on, to imagine Eve as a potential problem, despite the blissfulness with which 'hand in hand they pass'd, the lovliest pair / That ever since in love's embraces met' (Book 4, ll. 319–20).

Within a few pages, as we learn more about the 'Mother of Mankind' (Book 5, l. 388), she becomes even more problematic. In an apparently loving dialogue with Adam, Eve relates her memory of her birth from his rib: after she awakened she went to look at herself in a 'clear / Smooth lake' (Book 4, ll. 456–7) and was entranced by her own image, much like a female version of the mythical Greek Narcissus. When an airy voice warns her that 'What there thou seest fair Creature is thyself ... but follow me, / And I will bring thee' (Book 4, l. 466–68) to him 'whose image thou art' (Book 4, l. 470), she spies Adam and runs away, having thought him 'less fair ... Than that smooth wat'ry image' (Book 4, ll. 476–78) of herself. In fact, Adam has to remonstrate with her that she is 'His flesh, his bone' (Book 4, l. 481). Only after she surrenders herself to him, does she accept that beauty like hers is 'excell'd by manly grace / And wisdom, which alone is truly fair' (Book 4, ll. 488–89). Acknowledging that Adam is both her 'Author' and 'Disposer' (Book 4, l. 633), she proclaims that 'God is thy Law, thou mine: to know no more / Is woman's happiest knowledge and her praise' (Book 4, ll. 635–36). But Milton makes it even clearer that Eve is Adam's intellectual inferior. As Adam declares, God 'on her bestow'd' (Book 8, l. 537):

Too much of Ornament, in outward show
Elaborate, of inward less exact,
For well I understand in the prime end
Of Nature her th'inferior, in the mind
And inward Faculties. (Book 8, ll. 538–42)
In this way, Eve is more vulnerable than Adam to the
schemes of Satan. One night, 'Squat like a toad' (Book 4, l.
798), the fallen angel crouches by her ear and inspires her
with a prophetic dream in which she flies, witchlike, through
the sky and desirously views the forbidden tree, 'with fruit
surcharg'd' (Book 5, l. 58).[…]
Book 9: The serpent's temptation and Eve's rebellious
search for independence
Such bliss, as God points out to his Son, is not fated to last.

Satan, the high-ranking angel once known as Lucifer, Son of
the Morning, is enraged by his own secondariness to God's
Son and models rebellion to his followers and, ultimately, to
Eve. The ninth book of Paradise Lost presents the pivotal
moment when Milton's narrative metamorphoses from its
initial plan to discuss 'Man's First Disobedience', to an
analysis of woman's first disobedience. Here Satan creeps
again into Eden and resolves to disguise himself as a
serpent. But what a serpent! Gloriously phallic, the diabolic
creature appears not 'Prone on the ground, as since',

… but on his rear,
Circular base of rising folds, that tow'rd
Fold above fold a surging Maze, his Head
Crested aloft / … / pleasing was his shape,
And lovely. (Book 9, ll. 497–504)

After gaining her attention, he speaks with Machiavellian
eloquence to Eve, his intended prey.

How, though, has Eve happened to encounter him? As
Milton shows us, not by chance, but through her own
rebellious search for independence. Early in Book 9, as the
couple prepare to tend the Garden, she suggests to her

husband that they should 'divide our labours, thou where choice / Leads thee ... while I ... find what to redress till Noon' (Book 9, ll. 214–19). After all, she notes, when they work side-by-side, they waste too much time in loving discourse. Adam worries that harm will 'Befall thee sever'd from me' (Book 9, l. 252), for they must be on guard against a 'malicious Foe / Envying our happiness' (Book 9, ll. 253–54). The wife, he declares,

... where danger or dishonour lurks,
Safest and seemliest by her Husband stays,
Who guards her, or with her the worst endures. (Book 9, ll. 267–69)

But Eve disagrees, protesting that if she and her husband are forced 'to dwell / In narrow circuit strai'n'd by a Foe... How are we happy, still in fear of harm?' (Book 9, ll. 322–26). What kind of bliss can there be in Eden, she seems to be wondering, if she has so little freedom? Her urge to separate herself from Adam, if only briefly, is curiously reminiscent of the way in which she had run away from him after she was first created to be his spouse and 'second Self', and already prefigures doom.

Reason, resentment and rebellion: Eve's fall
Inevitably, as Eve journeys through the Garden on her own, Satan discovers her 'Veil'd in a cloud of Fragrance' (Book 9, l. 425) and begins his fatal seduction by praising her 'Celestial Beauty' (Book 9, l. 540). Astonished and not a little flattered, she wonders at his command of human speech: 'What may this mean? Language of Man pronounc't / By Tongue of Brute, and human sense exprest?' (Book 9, ll. 553–54). Now Satan embarks on his great temptation speech, which is almost like an operatic aria in praise of a certain 'goodly Tree' (Book 9, l. 576) that he doesn't name. Once he had eaten of it, he tells his naive listener, he experienced 'Strange alteration' (Book 9, l. 599), including 'Reason in my inward Powers, and Speech' (Book 9, l. 600).

The 'unwary' (Book 9, l. 614) Eve expresses an interest in seeing this amazing tree, and, of course, serpentine Satan leads her directly there. When she remonstrates that this tree bears the forbidden fruit, he embarks on another operatic aria praising its beneficence, to which she listens in all innocence. Beginning 'O Sacred, Wise, and Wisdom-giving Plant, / Mother of Science, Now I feel thy Power / Within me clear' (Book 9, ll. 679–81), he argues duplicitously that once she eats of this fruit she will be 'as Gods, / Knowing both Good and Evil as they know' (Book 9, ll. 708–09). His words 'Into her heart too easy entrance won' (Book 9, l. 734), since she is more susceptible to such wiles than Adam.

Or, alternatively, is Eve more ambitious, rebellious and disobedient than Adam? Milton leaves this question open. As Eve, reasoning (perhaps sophistically) with herself, notes that though the eating of the fruit supposedly brings death, 'How dies the Serpent? Hee hath eat'n and lives, / And knows and speaks, and reasons and discerns, / Irrational till then' (Book 9, ll. 764–66). In her soul she now appears as resentful, as Satan was before her. 'For us alone / Was death invented? Or to us denied / This intellectual food, for beasts reserv'd?' (Book 9, ll. 766–68). Satan has won the game, and Eve, in five succinct lines, determines to change the world:
… her rash hand in evil hour
Forth reaching to the Fruit, she pluck'd, she eat;
Earth felt the wound, and Nature from her seat
Sighing through all her works gave signs of woe,
That all was lost. (Book 9, ll. 780–84)
Now, though she has been 'eating Death' (Book 9, l. 792), she enters into a state of intoxication. '[J]ocund and boon' (Book 9, l. 793), she outlines an idolatrous plan to worship the Tree daily, then considers whether or not to share what she believes is her new divinity with her husband. Musing with an arrogance that parallels Satan's, she utters words that confirm her sinfulness, as she fantasises that she might,
…keeps the odds of Knowledge in my power

Without Copartner... so to add what wants
In Female Sex, the more to draw his Love,
And render me more equal, and perhaps
A thing not undesirable, sometime
Superior: for inferior who is free? [emphasis added] (Book 9,
ll. 820–25)

Ultimately, it's only the fear that God might have seen her
violation of His law that convinces her to offer the fruit to
Adam. For what if she died and were replaced with another
Eve? No, consumed with jealousy after her consumption of
forbidden knowledge, she decides it would be better for her
and Adam to die together. As for Adam, when she returns to
him bearing the fruit in her hand, he understands exactly
what has happened, mourning inwardly, 'How art thou lost,
how on a sudden lost, / Defac't, deflower'd, and now to
Death devote?' (Book 9, ll. 900–01). Yet, at the same time,
he resolves to die with her.

Love, lust and damnation: Adam's eating of the forbidden
fruit

If Eve's sin is (like Satan's) a rebellion against
secondariness, Adam's is his uxorious passion for Eve, his
lost rib, flesh of his flesh and bone of his bone. Accordingly,
although he 'scrupl'd not to eat' (Book 9, l. 997), he is 'not
deceiv'd, / But fondly overcome with Female charm' (Book 9,
l. 998–99). And while his forbidden meal damns him, it
doubly damns Eve, whose 'Female charm' is so insidious –
her 'wanton' locks paralleling the coils of the serpent – that
he can't resist her insistent pleas.

If a kind of drunkenness was Eve's first reaction to the fruit,
lust is Adam's, who finds her 'inflaming' (Book 9, l. 1013) his
senses and leads her, 'nothing loath' (Book 9, l. 1039), to a
shady bank. Where their earlier lovemaking had been
innocent and beautiful, their new fall into 'Love's disport' is
'of their mutual guilt the Seal, / the solace of their sin' (Book
9, ll. 1042–43). When they wake from a gross sleep, they
suddenly feel shame at their nakedness, 'destitute and bare
/ Of all their virtue' (Book 9, ll. 1062–63). Horrified, they fall
to blaming each other, and, tellingly, 'in mutual accusation

spent / The fruitless hours' [emphasis added] (Book 9, ll. 1187–88). For ultimately the fruit of the forbidden tree, as Satan and his cohort also discover in Hell, 'is dust and bitter ashes' (Book 10, The Argument).

Adam rejects the condolement of Eve'.
Redemption after transgression
What redemption can there be for Eve after her transgression? Gradually, throughout the last three books of Paradise Lost, Milton depicts her mounting remorse, shame and guilt. But by the end of the epic, once the Archangel Michael has revealed the coming history of mankind to Adam and, in sleep, to Eve, she is reconciled to her fate, understanding that 'By mee the Promise'd Seed shall all restore' (Book 11, l. 623): her descendant Mary shall become the Mother of God. Submissive, Eve is now a vessel for futurity. And though she and her husband have been expelled from Paradise, she assures Adam, in a poignant sonnet, that he means more to her than Eden:
With thee to go,
Is to stay here; without thee here to stay,
Is to go hence unwilling; thou to mee
Art all things under Heaven. (Book 11, ll. 615–18)
Her rehabilitation is secure so long as she abides by this vow, and according to Christian doctrine her 'willful crime' (Book 11, l. 619) shall come to be called a felix culpa – a fortunate fall – for it will bring God's Son to earth.
Eve's afterlife
How fortunate, though, was Eve's fall from the perspective of her countless female descendants? In A Vindication of the Rights of Women the pioneering feminist Mary Wollstonecraft passionately repudiated the infantilisation of women that she associated with Milton's description of 'our first frail mother'. In the 19th and 20th centuries, a number of important women writers fiercely lamented Eve's fall. In 'Eve', Christina Rossetti has our mythic first ancestress mourn that, 'As a tree my sin stands / To darken all lands' (ll. 5–6). And in 'How Cruel Is the Story of Eve', Stevie Smith struggles with a comparable burden, complaining 'How cruel

is the story of Eve, / What responsibility it has / In history /
For misery'. Unlike Rossetti, however, she emphasises
Eve's status as a fictive character:
It is only a legend
You say? But what
Is the meaning of the legend
If not
To give blame to women most
And most punishment?
Similarly, other modern and contemporary visions and re-
visions of Eve have emphasised her origin not as an
archetype, not as theological truth, but as a problematic
construction that is also an obstruction for women. As
Virginia Woolf wrote in the famously prophetic conclusion of
A Room of One's Own,
'if we look past Milton's Bogey ... then [the] dead poet who
was Shakespeare's sister will put on the body which she has
so often laid down'.
...that fair field Of Enna,
 where Prosérpine gath'ring flow'rs
Herself a fairer flow'r by gloomy
Dis Was gathered, which cost Ceres all that pain
 To seek her through the world...
 It is an astonishing leap out of a Christian world picture and
into a pagan, here taken from Ovid, who describes how
Proserpina, daughter of Ceres, the goddess of harvests, is
carried off by Dis, the god of the underworld, from Enna in
Sicily, and how Ceres searches for her and, failing to find
her, consigns the world to perpetual winter until her daughter
is restored to her; and the leap is accepted unhesitatingly by
the reader, who also understands that Proserpina is seen as
a version of Eve, another vulnerable and beautiful creature
attacked by a hellish predator.
Paradise Lost is full of these juxtapositions...
-         Clare Tomalin, Milton, Poems, p. XIII.
William Blake on John Milton, Paradise Lost:
"The reason Milton wrote in fetters when he wrote of Angels
& God, and at liberty when of Devils & Hell, is because he
was a true Poet and of the Devil's party without knowing it"

William Blake – another strong admirer of Milton's genius – modifies the difficulty in The Marriage of Heaven and Hell thus: The reason Milton wrote in fetters when he wrote of Angels & God, and at liberty when of Devils & Hell, is because he was a true Poet and of the Devils party without knowing it. Here Blake makes two points in one. First, that Milton's poetic imagination took flight when he wrote about Satan, but was constrained when he wrote of God and the angels, because Satan is essentially a subject better suited to poetry. Second, he also suggests that Milton was unaware of the effect to which he was victim.

'The want of human interest is always felt. Paradise Lost is one of the books which the reader admires and lays down and forgets to take up again. None ever wished it longer than it is. Its perusal is a duty rather than a pleasure. We read Milton for instruction, retire harassed and overburdened, and look elsewhere for recreation; we desert our master, and seek for companions.'
 - Samuel Johnson, "The Life of Milton"

William Wordsworth in The Prelude similarly imagined a lone, undaunted champion of virtue, "uttering odious truth, / Darkness before and danger's voice behind."23 In the sonnet "London, 1802," Wordsworth again depicts Milton as a solitary moral hero, whose "soul was like a Star, and dwelt apart."24 The poem's speaker beseeches Milton directly, "Milton! thou should'st be living at this hour: / England hath need of thee: she is a fen / Of stagnant waters" (lines 1 3). The speaker hopes that the author of Paradise Lost can rid England of its vanity "And give us manners, virtue, freedom, power" (line 8). Wordsworth apparently undertook his own epic The Prelude in part as a response to Milton's long poem, and other Romantic writers seem to have been similarly inspired by Milton's writings.25 Thus Mary Shelley in Frankenstein re-imagines Adam's divine creation through the characters of Victor and the Creature – Shelley even takes her novel's epigraph from Paradise Lost (X.743–45) – while Blake in his works reveals a lifelong fascination with

Milton's imagination and intellect. Not only did Blake paint two complete sets of watercolour illustrations for Paradise Lost but he also composed his own highly personal epic entitled Milton in which he envisions Milton's spirit returning to earth and communing personally with Blake's mind. In these works, Blake developed a nuanced and influential reading of Milton: while persisting in treating the God of Paradise Lost as a stern, moralistic patriarch, Blake recognized Satan's narcissism and came to view the Son as the epic's true hero.

Dobranski, Stephen B. The Cambridge Introduction to Milton (Cambridge Introductions to Literature) (pp. 199-200). Cambridge University Press. Kindle Edition.

'[Paradise Lost] contains within itself a philosophical refutation of that system of which, by a strange and natural antithesis, it has been a chief popular support.' - Shelley, A Defence of Poetry.

Percy Bysshe Shelley took a very different view. For him, Milton was very well aware of what he had done, and had done it with the intention of throwing down a gauntlet in the face of convention:

Milton's poem contains within itself a philosophical refutation of that system, of which, by a strange and natural antithesis, it has been a chief popular support. Nothing can exceed the energy and magnificence of the character of Satan as expressed in 'Paradise Lost.' It is a mistake to suppose that he could ever have been intended for the popular personification of evil... Milton's Devil as a moral being is as far superior to his God, as one who perseveres in some purpose which he has conceived to be excellent in spite of adversity and torture, is to one who in the cold security of undoubted triumph inflicts the most horrible revenge upon his enemy, not from any mistaken notion of inducing him to repent of a perseverance in enmity, but with the alleged design of exasperating him to deserve new torments. Milton has so far violated the popular creed... as to have alleged no superiority of moral virtue to his God over his Devil. And this

bold neglect of a direct moral purpose is the most decisive proof of the supremacy of Milton's genius.
 Shelley seems to wish here to package Milton as the pioneer of a revolutionary movement against authority and against convention – to make him a standard-bearer for Shelley himself. Satan here is no mere villain who has got out of hand: he is not only the most vivid character; he is first and foremost the moral hero of the poem. This character is very much Shelley's own Satan, and to that extent wildly distorted. From a more objective point of view, it is hard indeed to feel that Milton has not alleged moral superiority to God; he tells us in almost every line where God and Satan are opposed that God is superior; even Satan himself knowledges the fact.

'The civil war of the seventeenth century, in which Milton is a symbolic figure, has never been concluded. … Of no other poet is it so difficult to consider the poetry simply as poetry, without our theological and political dispositions, conscious and unconscious, inherited or acquired, making an unlawful entry.'
- T. S. Eliot, Milton (1947), p. 3.
In the twentieth century, critical opinion about Milton's style was dominated largely by T.S. Eliot's notorious theory of the 'dissociation of sensibility'8 – that is, the differentiation of thought and feeling, or of sense and sound – that he believed occurred in the seventeenth century. We can see echoes of this theory in the view of Grierson (outlined above) that Milton the thinker clashed with Milton the poet. Eliot approved the particularity of the Metaphysical poets such as John Donne, for whom, he asserted 'A thought... was an experience; it modified his sensibility'. Equally, he disapproved of the style of Milton as 'unsatisfactory', saying that 'His language is... artificial and conventional... Thus it is not so unfair, as it might at first appear, to say that Milton writes English like a dead language'.
- Edwards, Mike (2015) Paradise Lost: analysing texts.
The debate on Satan fuelled criticism for many years. By the time Grierson's Cross-Currents in the English Literature of

the XVIIth Century appeared in 1929 the debate had crystallised. Critics distinguished a moral poem from a poetic poem: according to this perception, Satan is poetically the most powerful character; in the moral structure, however, he nevertheless remains merely the antagonist – the temporarily successful but ultimately powerless antagonist – of mankind. For Grierson, 'There is no doubt that Satan is Milton's greatest creation' whose domination of the first two books 'far surpasses[es] in interest all that follows'.4 It is difficult to see Milton's poem as a success in the light of this perception, and – needless to say, perhaps – many have found cause to disagree with Grierson's assessment. What of the relationship between Adam and Eve? What of the portrait of the Garden of Eden? What of the temptation scene? What of the bitter aftermath of the Fall? What of the conclusion? Do these not at least bear comparison with the early books? These obvious reservations aside, Grierson's thesis is a persuasive one. Paradise Lost in his view expresses two Miltons: a poet, whose imaginative visions of Satan and the Garden and its inhabitants are richly drawn, and so compelling as to occupy the foreground of the poem as a whole; and, equally, a thinker whose thesis about justifying the ways of God to man constantly runs counter to, and tries to hold in check, the
more ebullient poetic material.
Edwards, Mike (2015) p, 205.

The other debate that dominated the study of Milton in the first half of the twentieth century focused less on Milton's poetic style and more on the depiction of God and Satan in Paradise Lost. Critics were divided about the sincerity of Milton's theodicy. According to one group, for which C. S. Lewis became the most eloquent spokesperson, the success of Milton's poem stemmed from its successful defence of divine justice. Lewis deemed the epic "overwhelmingly Christian" and asserted that, aside from "a few isolated passages," Paradise Lost does not reflect a particular set of beliefs but rather "gives the great central tradition."46 Thus, readers who object to Milton's God, Lewis concluded, "only mean that they dislike God."47 Another group of critics instead detected in Paradise Lost evidence of Milton's attraction to Satan and the author's own uncertainty about the Christian Deity. This tradition found probably its most influential voice in William Empson. Building on, as we have seen, Blake's Romantic suggestion that Milton was "of the Devil's party without knowing it," Empson argued that Milton in Paradise Lost was genuinely "searching" and "struggling to make his God appear less wicked," an attempt that Empson considered "the chief source" of the poem's "fascination and poignancy."48 To support Milton's sympathy for the devil, these critics could once again turn to the author's life, in particular his strident opposition to absolute kingship. Surely a poet who devoted so much time and energy to defending rebellion must have sympathized with Satan's passionate opposition to the monarchy of Heaven. In 1967 Stanley Fish deftly reconciled the two traditions by deploying the then burgeoning theoretical approach known as reader response criticism.49 He argued, in short, that both groups of critics – the Satanists and the orthodox Christians – were right. Placing the drama of the epic within the reader, Fish suggested that Milton didactically ensnares his audience with passages that make Satan look heroic and God seem wicked (Empson's perspective) so that Milton can then correct such a response by insisting on God's justice (Lewis's position). Readers thus repeatedly rediscover their own sinfulness as they are tempted to admire Satan's heroism – and then are admonished for not unquestioningly accepting divine obedience. But if Fish's reading of Satan's eloquence as a temptation for the reader continues to influence the teaching of Milton (and indeed grew out of Fish's own teaching at the University of Berkeley in the 1960s), the historical accuracy of Fish's theory has been effectively challenged and his representation of a punitive, Calvinist God in Paradise Lost has been dislodged.50 In describing the poem's effect, Fish, like many early practitioners of reader response criticism, posited an idealized, imaginary reader and overlooked the diversity of possible reactions that Milton's epic can prompt.

Flattening Paradise Lost into a single didactic manoeuvre, Fish's theory required readers who behaved as simpletons, repeatedly falling for the same trick, while it correspondingly distorted Milton into a finger-wagging pedant who takes almost sadistic glee in successively trapping and punishing the poem's fit audience. On the contrary, as John Rumrich has shown, Milton in his poetry and prose accepts doubt and indeterminacy as fundamental to human experience.51 And, as we have seen throughout this book, Milton in such diverse works as Areopagitica, Paradise Lost, and De Doctrina Christiana emphasizes the importance of interpretive freedom.

Dobranski, Stephen B.. The Cambridge Introduction to Milton (Cambridge Introductions to Literature) (pp. 203-204). Cambridge University Press. Kindle Edition.

Milton's note on the verse of Paradise Lost, added in the 1668 issue of the poem (and kept in subsequent editions), underscores his defensiveness and defiance as he writes in an insensitive age that may not adequately appreciate his daring literary achievements and ambitions. Clearly, many readers expected the poem, when it first appeared in 166 7, to rhyme. Rhyme, after all, was in fashion among royalist writers in the Restoration, especially for the heroic poem: Sir William Davenant had used rhyme in his uncompleted heroic poem Gondibert (1651), and other poets of the age, including Edmund mund Waller, John Dryden, and Abraham Cowley, used it as well. According to Aubrey, Dryden even asked Milton's permission "to put his Paradise Lost into a Drama in Rhyme" and Milton, receiving ing him graciously, wittily told the poet "he would give him leave to tagge his Verses" (Early Lives, p. 7). But in Paradise Lost, where Milton chooses blank verse, he follows the examples of his great classical precursors and originals - "Homer in Greek ... Virgil in Latin" - and consequently thinks rhyme is merely "the Invention of a barbarous Age, to set off wretched matter and lame Meter" (Hughes, p. 210).

David Loewenstein. Milton: Paradise Lost (Landmarks of World Literature (New)) (Kindle Locations 338-345). Kindle Edition.

Paradise Lost, then, does not present the visionary writer in a land of prophets and among the Lord's people engaged in energetic social reform (as does Areopagitica). Rather, the lonely prophet who published and partly wrote his poem in the politically "cold / Climate" (9.44-5) of the Restoration finds himself fall'n on evil days. On

-        David Loewenstein. Milton: Paradise Lost (Landmarks of World Literature (New)) (Kindle Locations 329-331). Kindle Edition.

One of the most pertinent prose texts for approaching Paradise Lost is Areopagitica (November 1644), Milton's famous attack on censorship. ship. A work in which Milton employs densely figurative prose to explore the ethical issues of confrontation, trial, and temptation, Areopagitica engages themes central to Paradise Lost, where Milton dramatizes issues of human choice and free will. Written in opposition sition to Parliament's Licensing Order of 1643, Areopagitica (itself addressed to Parliament, especially its more tolerant members) argues gues that certain forms of censorship will only hinder the ongoing ing process of reformation and social change. This process, Milton believes, is stimulated by the Revolution's ferment of new radical political and spiritual ideas, by the proliferation of religious sects, and by the outpouring of

-        David Loewenstein. Milton: Paradise Lost (Landmarks of World Literature (New)) (Kindle Locations 276-280). Kindle Edition.

In Milton's Tenure of Kings and Magistrates (1649) after the execution of Charles 1:

"No man who knows ought, can be so stupid to deny that all men naturally were borne free"

-        David Loewenstein. Milton: Paradise Lost (Landmarks of World Literature (New)) (Kindle Locations 262-263). Kindle Edition.

But in Paradise Lost, where Milton chooses blank verse, he follows the examples of his great classical precursors and originals - "Homer in Greek ... Virgil in Latin" - and consequently thinks rhyme is merely "the Invention of a barbarous Age, to set off wretched matter and lame Meter" (Hughes, p. 210).
David Loewenstein. Milton: Paradise Lost (Landmarks of World Literature (New)) (Kindle Locations 343-345). Kindle Edition.

Quotes from PL.
Milton knew he was writing something unique. After invoking both the Muse and the Holy Spirit, he continues that he was writing:
Things not attempted yet in Prose or Rhyme.'
Bk 1

From Milton, Paradise Lost Bk. IX [Adam], quoted by Mary Shelley in Frankenstein in part:
'O fleeting joyes
Of Paradise, deare bought with lasting woes! [...]
Did I request thee, Maker, from my Clay
To mould me Man, did I sollicite thee
From darkness to promote me, or here place
In this delicious Garden?
'Against his will he can receive no harm. But God left free the Will, or what obeys/Reason is free.'
P. L IX. 350-352.
'Formed them free, and free they must remain.'
    PL, III.124.
'Of Man's First Disobedience. '
P. L. 1.1.
' a paradise within.'
P. L. XII. 587. After the expulsion from Eden.
Satan: 'Better to reign in Hell, than to serve in Heaven.'
P. L 1.263.
Satan:
"The mind is its own place, and in itself / Can make a Heav'n of Hell, a Hell of Heav'n " (I.254–55),

Milton develops the character of Satan in Paradise Lost far beyond its biblical limitations:
'What though the field be lost?
All is not lost; the unconquerable will,
And study of revenge, immortal hate,
And courage never to submit or yield:
And what is else not to be overcome?

That glory never shall his wrath or might Extort from me.
To bow and sue for grace
With suppliant knee, and deify his power,
Who from the terror of this arm so late
Doubted his empire, that were low indeed,
That were an ignominy and shame beneath
This downfall.'
(P.L. I.105–16).
The mind is its own place, and in itself
 Can make a heaven of hell, a hell of heav'n.
What matter where, if I be still the same,
And what I should be, all but less than he
Whom thunder hath made greater? Here at least
We shall be free: th'Almighty hath not built
 Here for his envy, will not drive us hence:
 Here we may reign secure, and in my choice
To reign is worth ambition, though in hell;
Better to reign in hell than serve in heav'n.
–   Paradise Lost, Book One, lines 254-263.
Satan:
… pride and worse ambition threw me down
 Warring in Heav'n against Heav'n's matchless King:
 Ah wherefore! He deserved no such return
 From me, whom he created what I was
 In that bright eminence, and with his good
Upbraided none; nor was his service hard. (P.L. IV.40–45)

Other Quotes from PL:
Quote 1: Satan tells Beelzebub that "the mind is its own place, and in itself can make a
heav'n of hell, a hell of heav'n." Book 1, lines 254-5
Quote 2: Satan tries to make the best of the situation in hell, explaining "better to reign
in hell, than serve in heav'n." Book 1, line 263
Quote 3: Mammon advocates living to themselves in hell, "free, and to none
accountable, preferring hard liberty before the easy yoke of servile pomp." Book 2, lines
255-7

Quote 4: He advocates a new course of action: attack mortal man, who Beelzebub

describes as "less in power and excellence (than themselves), but favored more" by

God. Book 2, lines 349-50

Quote 5: Sin agrees to unlock the gates and let him pass, telling him "thou art my father,

thou my author, thou my being gav'st me; whom should I obey but thee, whom follow?"

Book 2, lines 864-5

Quote 6: God explains that he created man "sufficient to have stood, but free to fall."

Book 3, line 99

Quote 7: God describes the time of the Last Judgement, when the world will burn and

"God shall be all in all." Book 3, line 341

Quote 8: Uriel relates how, with God, "order from disorder sprung." Book 3, line 713

Quote 9: Satan, now back on earth, has a moment of doubt and despair in which he

says that "the hell I suffer seems a heav'n." Book 4, line 78

Quote 10: He notices that they are "both not equal, as their sex not equal seemed."

Book 4, lines 295-6

Quote 11: Satan explains that Adam's "eye sublime declared absolute rule." Book 4,

lines 300-1

Quote 12: He hears Adam tell Eve that they must not eat of the Tree of Knowledge,

calling it "the only sign of our obedience left," or else God will kill them. Book 4, line 428

Quote 13: Satan, having just learned that the Tree of Knowledge is forbidden to Adam

and Eve, ponders "ignorance, is that their happy state,/ the proof of their obedience and

their faith?" Book 4, lines 519-20

Quote 14: Soon, Adam decides that it's time to go to bed, and Eve obliges, stating "my author and disposer, what thou bidd'st unargued I obey." Book 4, lines 635-6

Quote 15: Before they fall asleep, Eve adds "God is thy law, thou mine: to know no

more is woman's happiest knowledge and her praise." Book 4, lines 637-8

Quote 16: Abdiel encounters Satan once again, this time telling him "I alone seemed in

thy world erroneous to dissent from all: my sect thou seest, now learn too late how few

sometimes may know, when thousands err." Book 6, lines 145-8

Quote 17: He tells Adam "warn thy weaker" (i.e., Eve), and "let it profit thee to have

heard by terrible example the reward of disobedience" Book 6, line 909-11

Quote 18: Milton makes his third invocation, this time to Urania, asking the goddess

what caused Adam and Eve to "transgress, and slight that sole command, so easily

obeyed amid the choice of all tastes else to please their appetite." Book 7, lines 47-9

Quote 19: After the people in this new world spend enough time being obedient, heaven

and earth will become "one kingdom, joy and union without end" Book 7, line 161

Quote 20: This divine figure calls himself the "author of all this thou seest above, or

round thee or beneath." Book 8, lines 317-8

Quote 21: Adam has not received a true equal, however; he explains that Eve is "th'

inferior, in the mind and inward faculties." Book 8, lines 541-2

Quote 22: Milton starts this book on a melancholy note, informing the reader that he

must "change these notes to tragic; foul distrust, and breach disloyal on the part of man,

revolt and disobedience." Book 9, lines 5-8

Quote 23: He explains "only in destroying I find ease to my restless thoughts." Book 9,
lines 129-30

Quotes 24: Adam replies that God made them "not to irksome toil, but to delight." Book
9, line 242

Quotes 25: Adam says, "solitude sometimes is best society, and short retirement urges
sweet return." Book 9, lines 249-50

Quote 26: He asks "Wherein lies th'offense, that man should thus attain to know?" Book
9, lines 725-6

Quote 27: Oblivious Eve is thrilled to have received knowledge, and wonders whether
she should let Adam partake in it or not tell him and keep it to her advantage so to
"render [herself] more equal." Book 9, line 825

Quote 28: The Son asks Adam if Eve was his God or superior, since his "perfection far
excelled hers in all real dignity." Book 10, line 150-1

Quote 29: Secondly, woman is given pain in childbirth, and the Son explains "to thy
husband's will thine shall submit, he over thee shall rule." Book 10, lines 195-6.

Quote 30: Finally, man gets his punishment: he'll have to toil hard in the fields to get
food "till thou return into the ground, for thou out of the ground wast taken: know thy
birth, for dust thou art, and shalt to dust return." Book 10, lines 206-8

Quote 31: She says "these are thy magnific deeds, thy trophies, which thou view'st as
not thine own, thou art their author and prime architect." Book 10, lines 354-6

Quote 32: He asks God "Why has thou added the sense of endless woes? Inexplicable thy justice seems." Book 10, lines 753-5

Quote 33: She says "both have sinned, but thou against God only, I against God and

thee." Book 10, lines 930-1
Quote 34: Michael tells Adam, "you have seen one world begin and end and man as from a second stock proceed." Book 12, line 7
Quote 35: Michael says, "the law of God exact he shall fulfill/ both by obedience and by love." Book 12, lines 403-4
Quote 36: A teary Adam and Eve await their future: "the world was all before them, where to choose/ their place of rest, and Providence their guide:/ They hand in hand with wand'ring steps and slow,/ Through Eden took their solitary way." Book 12, lines 646-9

Notes on Joseph Conrad .
General criticism.
These first four ' close readings' have to be particularly rigorous as the texts, 1) The Moonstone, 2) Heart of Darkness, 3) Paradise Lost and 4) Anita Desai's complete short stories will be referenced in teaching throughout the first year of this new MA in English Literature. There are also another nine books, but you have an element of choices regarding them.

Heart of Darkness is undoubtedly Modernist in its Form. But the text is deeply disturbing and, is therefore, correctly, critiqued from a Post colonialist perspective.

He is interested in having discovered that Joseph Conrad called himself: a 'homo duplex.' a double man. He now understands where Terry Eagleton derived his account of Conrad as a 'man of contradictions'. This is apparent in Lord Jim, The Secret Agent and Heart of Darkness. Marlow is the protagonist in Youth, Lord Jim and Heart of Darkness.

It is worth realising that Conrad knew Roger Casement, whose (1904) 'Congo Report' turned public opinion against slavery in the Congo under the so-called 'Noble Mission' of King Leopold II. The British State would later execute Sir Roger Casement for his involvement in the Easter Uprising of 1916. Conrad wrote Heart of Darkness in many manuscripts. For example, the original 1898-99 serial edition has 'Oh, the Horror. ' As opposed to the 1902 book version, famously 'The Horror, the horror. ' Yet some authorities argue for the source derived from a 1921 edition. The point is that texts are mutable.

"Did he live his life again in every detail of desire, temptation, and surrender during that supreme moment of complete knowledge? He cried in a whisper at some image, at some vision—he cried out twice, a cry that was no more than a breath— "'The horror! The horror!''
-          Joseph Conrad, Heart of Darkness. Norton, p. 69.
"His was an impenetrable darkness. I looked at him as you peer down at a man who is lying at the bottom of a precipice where the sun never shines."
- Conrad, Joseph. Heart of Darkness (Penguin Classics) (p. 50). Penguin Books Ltd. Kindle Edition. Marlow commenting on Kurtz,

Unfortunately, Virginia Woolf avoids 'Heart of Darkness' in her essay on Conrad for the TLS. However, she does argue that, generally, it was: "Marlow who comments, Conrad who creates. " Also, there is no mention of 'The Secret Agent.' Correctly, she writes about Conrad's "double life, for Conrad was composed of two men, she comments." This is a recurrent theme in Anglophone criticism. Conrad had described himself as a 'Homo Duplex,' a double man.

Postcolonial criticism.

Chinua Achebe's (1977) An Image of Africa offersrs a well-argued counter-discursive or resistant reading of Heart of Darkness.
Conrad 'parodies in the most vulgar fashion, prejudices and insults from which a selection of mankind has suffered untold agonies and atrocities in the past and continues to do so in many places today. I am talking about a story in which the very humanity of black people is called into question. (in Hammer, 1990, pp.124, 126).
Joseph Conrad's Heart of Darkness, quoted in Edward W. Said 'Culture and Imperialism:'
'The conquest of the earth, which mostly means the taking it away from those who have a different complexion or slightly flatter noses than ourselves, is not a pretty thing when you look into it too much. What redeems it is the idea only. An idea at the back of it; not a sentimental pretence but an idea; and an unselfish belief in the idea—something you can set up, and bow down before, and offer a sacrifice to ....'

'Marlow repeats and confirms Kurtz's action: restoring Africa to European Hegemony by historicising and narrating its strangeness.
Edward Said, Culture and Imperialism, p. 198.

'The power to narrate, or to block other narratives from forming and emerging, is very important to culture and imperialism and constitutes one of the main connections between them. Most important, the grand narratives of mobilised and enlightenment mobilized people in the colonial world to rise up and throw off imperial subjection; in the process, many Europeans and Americans were also stirred by these stories and their protagonists, and they, too, fought for new narratives of equality and human community.'
Edward W. Said (1994) Culture & Imperialism.
'Readers of this book will quickly discover that narrative is crucial to my argument here, my basic point being that stories are at the heart of what explorers and novelists say

about strange regions of the world; they also become the method colonised people use to assert their own identity and the existence of their history. The primary battle in imperialism is over land, of course. Still, when it came to who owned the land, who had the right to settle and work on it, who kept it going, who won it back, and who now plans its future—these issues were reflected, contested, and even for a time decided in narrative'.
Edward W. Said (1994) Culture & Imperialism.

Sustained reading. Conrad's prose is sometimes quite complex and, on occasion, sympathetic to the black people, to the plight of the oppressed around Marlow. However, it is peppered with the N-word. I suggest this provides evidence for Edward W. Said's (1994) 'Two Visions in the Heart of Darkness' and their incompatibility.
See Said (1994), p. 20-35.

Marxist criticism.

Terry Eagleton (2005) The English Novel
'As reality is bleached of value, so the human psyche begins
to implode. What we are left with is a human being who is
valuable but unreal, in a world which is solid but valueless.
Meaning and value are driven from the public world, which is
now just a soulless expanse of neutral facts, and thrust deep
into the interior of the human subject, where they all but
vanish. The world is thus divided down the middle between
fact and value, public and private, and object and meaning.
This, for Georg Lukács in Theory of the Novel, is the
alienated condition of the modern age, which the novel
reflects in its inmost form.'
Eagleton (2005), p.18.

Terry Eagleton (2005) The English Novel.
How can you tell a story in such a situation? It seems less
and less possible to pluck a narrative from a world of lifeless,
disconnected objects. So the novelist can turn instead to the
inner life. But this life has been driven in upon itself, beating
a retreat from a soulless world; and it has become so subtle
and densely textured in the process that it resists anything
as straitjacketing and steamrollering as narrative. We shall
see this in the sentences of the later Henry James, which try
to say everything at once without simply log jamming. So the
external world is becoming too poor for narrative, and the
internal one too rich. Narratives of the inner world are a
problem because the human psyche no longer seems a
linear affair, as it did when what mattered was who your
ancestors were and whether you would transmit their beliefs
intact to your own children. Instead, it is a place where past,
present and future interlock, with no clear frontiers between
them. Nor will the inner life provide you with any sure way of
distinguishing between what is significant and what is not,
since what both have in common is that they happen to you.
The interior monologues of Leopold and Molly Bloom in
Joyce's Ulysses are a case in point. This deepens the

general crisis of value, as all experiences seem to be mixed promiscuously together.

For Lukács, then, the novel is the product of an alienated world. Yet it is also a utopian response to it. Alienation is the condition in which men and women fail to recognize the objective world as their own subjective creation. Yet the very act of writing a novel offers an alternative to this condition, since a novel's 'objective' vision of the world is one rooted in the subjectivity of its author. The act of writing crosses the border between subjective and objective. The novel is one of the few objects in a reified society which manifests in its every objective detail the subjective freedom in which it was born. In this sense, its very existence can be seen as an imaginary solution to the social problems which it poses. The situation which Lukács depicts in Theory of the Novel is truer of the twentieth-century modernist novel than of the nineteenth-century realist one. The great works of nineteenth-century realism, from Pride and Prejudice to Middlemarch, are still able to relate fact and value, objective and subjective, inner and outer, individual and society, however much these relations may be under strain. As such, they spring from a buoyant, dynamic episode of middle-class history. It is this history which Lukács's later work on literary realism is concerned to investigate. It is only when middle-class civilization enters upon a major crisis, one which is at its height from the close of the nineteenth century to the end of the First World War, that literary modernism arises, and the novel shifts from being a primarily comic to a predominantly tragic form. Then, indeed, the early Lukács's description of the novel form becomes more and more apt. It is an art which can no longer shape the contradictions which plague it into a coherent whole. Instead, as we shall see in the case of authors like Henry James and Joseph Conrad, those conflicts are now beginning to infiltrate the very form of the novel itself. They reflect themselves in the break-up of language, the collapse of narrative, the unreliability of reports, the clash of subjective standpoints, the fragility of value, the elusiveness of overall meaning. 'Organic form' is now so unattainable, or so flagrantly arbitrary, that it is either

thrown to the winds or, as with a work like James Joyce's Ulysses, grotesquely parodied. The modern world is too fragmentary for the novel to mould it into a totality; but it is also because there is simply too much of it, too many specialist jargons and domains of knowledge, that this is no longer feasible. What the modernist novel tends to give us instead is a kind of empty signifier of a totality which is no longer possible: the silver of Conrad's Nostromo, Stevie's scribbled circles in The Secret Agent, E. M. Forster's Marabar caves, Virginia Woolf's lighthouse. The realist novel represents one of the great revolutionary cultural forms of human history. In the domain of culture, it has something like the importance of steam-power or electricity in the material realm, or of democracy in the political sphere. For art to depict the world in its everyday, unregenerate state is now so familiar that it is impossible to recapture its shattering originality when it first emerged. In doing so, art finally returned the world to the common people who had created it through their labour, and who could now contemplate their own faces in it for the first time. A form of fiction had been born in which one could be proficient without specialist erudition or an expensive classical education. As such, it was especially available to groups like women, who had been cheated of such an education and shut out from such expertise.
Eagleton (2005) The English Novel. P. 18-20.

Conrad was equally typical of traditionalist England in his hatred of socialism ('infernal doctrines born in the continental backslums'), his disgust with democracy ('I have no taste for democracy'), and his patronizing attitude to the common people ('For the great mass of mankind, the only saving grace that is needed is steady fidelity to what is nearest to hand and heart'). He despised the notion of equality, detested the liberal values of pity, sentiment, pacificism and humanitarianism (we shall see a similar aversion in D. H. Lawrence), and harboured a Baden-Powellish belief in the virtues of discipline, deference, fidelity, male bonding and an unthinking respect for authority and tradition. His women

characters, with one or two admirable exceptions, are sketchy or embarrassing stereotypes.
Eagleton, Terry. The English Novel (pp. 233-234). Wiley. Kindle Edition.

This shadowy self in Conrad is by no means a simple-hearted English Tory. On the contrary, it is a full-blooded Continental sceptic, influenced by the thought of philosophers like Schopenhauer and Nietzsche. In what is scarcely the cheeriest of viewpoints, Conrad would seem to hold that personal identity is an illusion, truth and meaning eternally elusive, language fundamentally inadequate, human consciousness an unhappy accident, and Nature a meaningless, impenetrable chaos. History is a futile cycle of violence and savagery, progress is a chimera, civilization is a higher form of barbarism, and egoism is the underlying truth of human conduct. Motivations for action are arbitrary and irrational, and action itself a gross simplification of the unfathomable complexity of the world and the self.
Eagleton, Terry. The English Novel (p. 235). Wiley. Kindle Edition.

Much of this is off-the-peg nineteenth-century irrationalism. But it is also the ideology of the exile, one whose sense of identity has been undermined early on by the burden of an imperial autocracy, and who has lived through a profound historical crisis at the heart of Europe. Conrad belongs to a European history which, as it approaches the turn of the twentieth century, is moving out of its more buoyant, affirmative phase, with its belief in the free, self-determining individual, into a darker, more downbeat civilization altogether. The capitalist system has been pitched into the prolonged economic slump which will play its part in 1914 in staging history's first global imperialist war.
Eagleton, Terry. The English Novel (p. 235). Wiley. Kindle Edition.
In terms of literary form, this is reflected in a running battle between romance and realism. Imperialism is a form of Romantic idealism, with its flag-waving rhetoric of God and

nation and its vision of a transformed earth. But it is an idealism motivated by a less than godly materialism. The ship's deck is the thin partition between the two, separating the idealized comradeship of the crew from the profitable commercial

Eagleton, Terry. The English Novel (p. 236). Wiley. Kindle Edition.

goods in the hold. You can then, as in Conrad's fiction, celebrate the hard work, loyalty and conscientiousness on deck while forgetting the material ends which all this ultimately serves. There are other contradictions as well. Imperialism demands faith, resolute action and an unswerving belief in one's own values. But it also brings you into contact with other cultures which are different from your own, but which seem despite this lamentable misfortune to be in reasonable working order. Such encounters are then bound to raise awkward questions about the absoluteness of one's own way of life. In doing so, they threaten to subvert one's sense of supremacy at exactly the point where it is most urgently needed. Imperialism breeds a disabling cultural relativism. By Conrad's time, the liberal, humanistic values which had served the West so splendidly in its earlier, more self-assured historical phase are being called into question, by Yeats, Freud, T. S. Eliot, Ezra Pound, Martin Heidegger and D. H. Lawrence as much as by the ferociously anti-Enlightenment Pole. Reason and progress have been unmasked as a lie, truth and objectivity exposed as delusions, and on all sides there is a return to the mythical and primitive, savage gods and mystical archetypes.

Eagleton, Terry. The English Novel (p. 236). Wiley. Kindle Edition.

Values and beliefs may have no sure grounding in a random evolutionary universe; but by clinging tenaciously to our ideals, whether they are represented by the Koran or a standard of seamanlike conduct, we confer meaning and order on our inherently pointless lives. And for this purpose, any ideal will really do. What matters is not so much the content of our beliefs as the passionate intensity with which

we stay faithful to them. It is an ethic which is on the turn, so to speak, from Romanticism to existentialism. You must live fictionally, hypothetically, as if your values had an unimpeachable basis. It is in this way that full-blown sceptics like Martin Decoud of Nostromo can be worsted.
Eagleton, Terry. The English Novel (pp. 236-237). Wiley. Kindle Edition.

All these in Conrad are questions of literary form, not just of content. What strikes one about his prose is how it manages to be vivid and concrete yet ambiguous and equivocal. In this mixture of the immediate and the intangible, his writing has the quality of a dream, which seems both more and less intense than waking life. Indeed, Conrad often sees human existence as a kind of dream. The typical Conradian story is a colourful tale of action and adventure, surrounded by a misty penumbra of elusive meanings. One critic aptly describes Heart of Darkness as 'a detective story gone modernist'.1 If the focus is too firmly on the narrative, the tale loses its 'artistic' evocativeness; but if we delve too deeply into the surrounding mist, the solidity of the narrative might be undermined. The storyline of Heart of Darkness threatens constantly to dissolve into a montage of static, dream-like tableaux. Yet one has to stay faithful to the evanescent meanings which flicker round the story's margins, just as one has to keep faith with an elusive Other like Jim or Kurtz. The conflict in Conrad between 'difficult' modernist and Boys Own aventure writer is a formal version of the conflict between sceptical émigré and English conservative. If Conrad's prose is visually graphic and finely sculptured, it is not at all because he has a robust faith in the powers of language. It is rather because, like many a modernist writer, he has exceedingly little. Every word and meaning, he once remarked, floats in a sea of doubts and indeterminacies. To be valid, language must stay close to one's sensations, which for Conrad are more trustworthy than the alienated intellect. But sensations are also notoriously deceptive and impressionistic. If the prose of the novels is so meticulously wrought, it is partly because their author regards language as threadbare and duplicitous. It

113

shares in what he sees as the dismal inauthenticity of everyday social life. Language faces outwards towards the light, but at the same time gestures inwards towards an inexpressible darkness.

Eagleton, Terry. The English Novel (pp. 237-238). Wiley. Kindle Edition.

If colonialism is to be criticized, it is among other things because it, too, imagines like the storyteller that it can impose order on a formless world. It tries to hammer disorderly peoples into unity, lick them into shape. The fact that this enterprise is fruitless is a compliment neither to the colonizers nor to the colonized. It suggests that the former are obtuse and the latter are inherently unruly. Something of the same ambiguity can be found in E. M. Forster's A Passage to India. The imperial invaders are discredited, but not in a way which particularly flatters the natives.
Eagleton, Terry. The English Novel (p. 238). Wiley. Kindle Edition.

Discovering the truth is a matter of finding a form, recounting a story; yet in doing so one finds oneself sculpting a void, since the world itself no longer constitutes a coherent narrative. Just as history displays no built-in progress, so there is no longer any credence to be placed in the shapely unfolding of a tale. The truth is no longer narratable. You will not disclose it, as George Eliot trusted one might, by patiently unravelling the chains of cause and effect. Chronology is no longer any reliable guide to reality. Time and space are just cultural constructs to which the world itself is utterly indifferent. All you can hope to do, then, is come at the truth now from one angle and now from another, slicing in and out of the story, skating backwards and forwards in time. You can loop, suspend and replay your narrative until it might just yield you the ghost of a truth – a truth that is not itself historical or orderly, and which can be shown rather than stated. In fact, storytelling involves a double falsehood, since reality is itself shot through with illusion, and the act of trying to communicate this in language is equally distorting. When Marlow in Heart of Darkness finally hears what he persuades himself is the pure voice of truth, one which will give his journey meaning, it is merely Kurtz's cry 'The horror, the horror'. The 'final' word is empty, negative, absent. As a modern theorist might put it, there is no transcendental signifier, but it is the fruitless search for it which makes narrative possible. Any particular story-line is bound to be arbitrary, just as Marlow's voyage in Heart of Darkness is gratuitous and unmotivated. In any case, even if truth can be discovered, it is not clear that there is anyone out there to receive it. The Marlow of Heart of Darkness is quite literally delivering his tale in the dark, unable to see his audience as he squats on deck. It is a graphic image of the problems of the modernist writer and his or her dwindling, anonymous readership.

Eagleton, Terry. The English Novel (pp. 238-239). Wiley. Kindle Edition.

Heart of Darkness turns on Kurtz, who is seen and heard only obliquely, and his unseen unspeakable rites; while at the centre of...Kurtz also has a hollowed centre, like the place he occupies in the tale.

Eagleton, Terry. The English Novel (p. 239-240). Wiley. Kindle Edition.

Some things and characters in Conrad are unfathomable because they are swathed in obscurity, and some because there is nothing there to be known. Is the heart of Africa dark because we Westerners cannot penetrate it, or is it dark, so to speak, inherently? Is it meaningless in itself, or simply obscure from our standpoint? Is it the thing itself which is askew, or our way of seeing it? Is there an 'objective' chaos and horror there, or is it just a case of our blurred vision? How can something which has no meaning in the first place be said to be inscrutable?

Eagleton, Terry. The English Novel (p. 240). Wiley. Kindle Edition.

If colonialism is a false imposition of order on chaos, then one might expect Conrad to be straightforwardly opposed to it. But little in Conrad is straightforward. Narrative is also a falsifying sort of order, but it is indispensable even so. The anti-imperialist aspects of Heart of Darkness are evident enough in, say, Marlow's withering remarks about those who snatch land from those who have slightly flatter noses than ourselves. But there is also something disturbing about the tale's presentation of imperialism. It is not just the reach-me-down racism of its portraits of 'natives', or its apparent endorsement of British as opposed to Belgian colonization. It is also that the whole imperialist enterprise is represented as essentially absurd. It is a surreally pointless exercise, symbolized by a ship firing purposelessly into a river bank, a pail with a hole in it, a hollow in the ground excavated for no apparent purpose, a man weirdly garbed in motley, and a chief accountant conducting himself in the middle of the jungle as he might in an English drawing-room. All this makes for powerful dramatic effect; but it also suggests that imperialism is simply a kind of irrational fantasy, a waking nightmare or absurdist theatre, which is far from being the case. On the contrary, nothing could be more grimly rational, at least in one rather anaemic sense of the word. There is nothing in the least futile or unreal about sailing in, massacring the inhabitants, grabbing their raw resources and sailing out again. In the period between Conrad's own visit to the Congo in 1890, and the First World War, millions of Africans were slaughtered by European imperial powers for hard-headed political and economic reasons. Imperialism is not in the least pointless. Indeed, the much-quoted passage in Heart of Darkness which describes the ship firing its guns into the jungle concludes with the suggestion that there is indeed a hostile camp of 'natives' around the place, so that the assault is perhaps not quite so 'insane' after all. Conrad pulls his narrative back within the protective limits of realism just in time. He does, however, harbour the belief, typical of some right-wing thought of the time, that beneath all apparently purposeful public action lie irrational private motives; and we shall see this view writ large in Nostromo.

As a result, imperialism is seen in Heart of Darkness not as a purposeful, historically intelligible system, but as a kind of nightmarish aberration. The difference between right-wing irrationalism and capitalist imperialism is a vital one to the understanding of Conrad's political attitudes. What he dislikes about imperialism, quite apart from its greed and brutality, is that it is supposedly inspired by enlightened ideals of reason, progress, altruism, peace, prosperity, civilization and the like, ideals which he despises. As a right-wing irrationalist, Conrad believes instead in the realities of egoism, barbarism and eternal conflict, the frailty of reason and the relative unimportance of such mundane matters as prosperity. He also suspects that history, far from progressing, is actually slipping backwards into savagery. So his views give no comfort to imperialism; but neither do they lend support to its left-wing opponents. The leading critics of imperialism of Cornad's age were political radicals who believed, not without reason, that history could be more than barbarism; that social improvement, however arduous, was possible, and had taken place in the past; and that human action was governed by more than egoism. These men and women held that a reasoned analysis of the colonialist system was vital to the fight against it; that only the privileged can afford to scoff at issues of material prosperity; and that civilization need not be in an eternal state of warfare. It is important to see, then, that Kurtz in Heart of Darkness is a left-winger, or at least was when he first came to Africa, which is one reason why Conrad detests him so much. Those 'unspeakable rites' and secret abominations arc among other things Conrad's revenge on social reformers. Scratch a humanitarian and you find a monster. Kurtz is an 'emissary of pity, and science, and progress, and devil knows what else',
Eagleton, Terry. The English Novel (pp. 241-243). Wiley. Kindle Edition.
who would have made a good politician 'on the popular side', and who has a formidable capacity for populist rhetoric. In acting out the degradation of Kurtz, then, Heart of Darkness is not only exposing the real rapacity which lurks

beneath high-sounding imperial ideals; it is also seeking to discredit the leftists who did most to challenge that predatory system. In this way, it can win for itself the best of both political worlds, spurning the greedy middle-class commercialists and colonialists (for whom Conrad anyway feels a patrician disdain), while also rebuffing their radical opponents. Instead, it advances a more scandalous, tough-minded revelation than either camp is supposedly capable of: beneath imperialism lies the eternal barbarousness of the human condition. What is awry is not political history but the human heart. This makes the whole situation more dramatic and deep-rooted, but only at the cost of rendering it unalterable. If it is true, there seems little that can be done about the imperialist system – a message which is more welcome to its champions than to its critics. Besides, if the nihilists are right and human values are a sham, then there would seem no more reason not to exploit Africans than to do so. And if enslaving Africans is simply the effect of original sin, it may be as natural and inevitable as it is regrettable.

Eagleton, Terry. The English Novel (p. 243). Wiley. Kindle Edition.

In the end, so Heart of Darkness suggests, high-flown ideals and fancy sentiments will never save us from the persistent fact of savagery. Such ideals, like human civilization itself, are only skin-deep. Civilization is merely a subtle form of barbarism; in fact, it is in some ways worse than actual barbarism, since to live it out self-consciously, as the decadent Kurtz does, is to exacerbate it. All moderns are cannibals in thin disguise. Our brutishness persists beneath the skin, as Marlow recognizes when Kurtz's supposed primitivism evokes in him an appalled affinity. Civility, in what one might call the Lord of the Flies syndrome, is precariously paper-thin, and we can regress from it at any moment to our bestial origins. As Marlow's story and journey press forward, they simultaneously drift backward into a primitive past which civilization has never really abandoned. Conservative, pessimistic seafarers like Conrad and Golding are out to persuade us that there is no faith to be placed in human culture or history. With Golding, the message has a theological twist in its tail. The only issue in the end is whether we, like Kurtz, have the courage to confess that we are at heart savages as well. As well as who, though? It is surely something of a back-handed compliment to inform the inhabitants of Borneo or the Congo that we are quite as brutal and bloodthirsty as they are. Is this supposed to make them feel better?

Eagleton, Terry. The English Novel (pp. 243-244). Wiley. Kindle Edition.

It is hard not to suspect that the Marlow of Heart of Darkness is a touch deranged. His account is so coloured, hyperbolic and latently hysterical as to be only dubiously reliable…It is hard not to suspect that the Marlow of Heart of Darkness is a touch deranged. His account is so coloured, hyperbolic and latently hysterical as to be only dubiously reliable. Either that, or Conrad's own writing here is remarkably garish and lurid, with nothing like the supple leanness of the prose of Nostromo. Perhaps one could try reading the tale like Henry James's 'The Turn of the Screw', as an apparently reliable story delivered by a deluded narrator. So much in the book seems to be relentlessly dragooned into generating an ominous 'atmosphere', in a kind of verbal overkill or visual equivalent of melodrama. Take, for example, this description of a woman's expression: 'Her face had a tragic and fierce aspect of wild sorrow and of dumb pain mingled with the fear of some struggling, half-shaped resolve'. Trying to imitate this ludicrously complicated expression, which exists almost purely at the level of language, would be a useful exercise for a drama school, if a dispiriting one. Marlow has only to hear the innocuous names of some African villages to feel that they 'belong to some sordid farce acted in front of a sinister back-cloth', and this before anything even faintly sinister has even happened. He is grimly set on whipping up a sensational drama out of a minor incident, and has only to see some Africans wandering harmlessly around to feel a 'taint of imbecile rapacity' in the air. His steamer is not allowed simply to travel along the river bank; instead, it must toil

Eagleton, Terry. The English Novel (p. 244). Wiley. Kindle Edition.

along 'the edge of a black and incomprehensible frenzy'. An African cannot step casually into the jungle without the wilderness having taken him again to its bosom. The whole thing is contrived, heavy-handed, laboriously unreal, and very much as though Marlow is seeing what he is at all costs determined to see. If this were not a fiction, it would cry out for comparison with someone else's account of the whole affair. The constant emphasis on the mystery and genius of Kurtz is another rather flat-footed device, since it is clear enough that this image is being generated only to be deflated. There is very little hard evidence to back up this breathless reverence, just as there is precious little to support Lord Jim's receiving as much fascinated attention as the novel lavishes on him. Kurtz is an early example of a kind of character we encounter often enough in modern fiction: one who is commended not so much for what he says or does, but for pushing himself to an extreme, staying faithful to the truth of himself, and living out his desires to the full. With Kurtz and his ilk, we have moved deep into the Romantic or existential cult of 'authenticity'. What matters, for this deeply suspect doctrine, is the sheer intensity of your commitment, not its actual content. What counts is going all the way, not so much the direction in which you are headed. Whereas others live a timorously conventional existence, these modern heroes are prepared to break through the thin veneer.

Eagleton, Terry. The English Novel (pp. 244-245). Wiley. Kindle Edition.

Like Dickens, Conrad often makes his point by the disreputable technique of caricaturing those he disapproves of.

Eagleton, Terry. The English Novel (p. 251). Wiley. Kindle Edition.

'The loss of reality has become a central problem in the highly industrialized late capitalist world. '
  - Ernst Fischer (1963) The Necessity of Art: A Marxist Approach p. 197.
Organic intellectuals shape and encourage the growth of:
"New popular beliefs, that is to say a new common sense and with it a new culture and a new philosophy which will be rooted in the popular consciousness with the same solidity and imperative quality as traditional beliefs" (Gramsci 1971, p. 424).
Contradistinguished from the "traditional intellectuals" who supply ideological legitimation of the status quo, the organic intellectuals in the ranks of the proletariat are class-conscious communists.
Barbara Foley, Marxist Literary Criticism Today. p. 79

On John Clare, labouring class poetics, patronage, grammar, and madness:

A Gramscian analysis.

Some positional quotations.

An assertion made by Wordsworth about Chatterton and Burns in the poem Resolution and Independence:

We poets in our youth begin in gladness.
But thereof comes in the end despondency and madness
(William Wordsworth, Resolution and Independence, 1802)

Clare emerges for readers in this society as a displaced, marginalized poet whose reputation is gradually being rehabilitated. . ... But it could be that Clare—shy, feral, intensely gifted—will never be redeemed from all the neglect and mutilation he has suffered.

People expect originality... The truth is, prisons and manicomi (mental institutes), are packed with original types. Nevertheless, every revolutionary has originality.

Marx has not written a catechism; he is not a messiah who left a string of parables laden with categorical imperatives of absolute, indisputable norms outside the categories of time and space. The only categorical imperative, the only norm, is: 'Workers of the world unite.'

...his way of viewing things is not a doctrine but a method. It does not provid ready-made dogmas, but criteria for further research.

the philosophy of praxis is consciousness full of contradictions, in which the philosopher himself, understood both individuality and as an entire group, not merely grasps the contradictions, but posits himself as an element of the contradictions and elevates this element to a principle of knowledge and therefore of action. .

Who has really attempted to follow up the explorations of Marx and Engels? I can only
think of Gramsci.

Gramsci says of Dostoyevsky's work that it shows 'an awareness that the intellectuals have a mission towards the people'. Gramsci continues, 'The people may be "objectively" made up of the "humble" but they must be freed from this "humility", transformed and regenerated.

Clare's place in the tradition of English literature cannot be established by
simple chronology or solely by reference to the leading writers of his age,
though he was born just one year later than Shelley and lived until a year
before Yeats was born. Since Clare continued to write from his adolescence
until a few years before his death, he belongs chronologically to the age of
Blake, Bloomfield, Scott, Crabbe, Coleridge, Byron, Shelley, Keats and
Wordsworth.

it was taken for granted that a peasant poet was uneducated in a deliberateand specializing sense. Being uneducated implied a lack of the knowledge of formal grammar, yet at the same time it ensured a power to break through established conventions, a freshness and a spontaneity of observation and feeling, the qualities that had supposedly been lost in the movement to a more artificial way of life and culture.

This thesis will contend that a reading of John Clare is enhanced by the employment of a Gramscian methodology and that this advances the scholarship of Clare. Following the logic of Historical Materialism, Antonio Gramsci's central concepts, such as Traditional and Organic intellectuals,

Hegemony, and, therefore, counter-hegemonic intellectuals, cannot be understood as abstractions outside of the class struggle but should, instead, be applied to the 'lived experience' of concrete people and 'sensory activity.' Thus, I shall examine several areas in John Clare's concrete experience, considering Gramsci's key concepts. My first task is to position Gramscian theory and my argument in the intertextual narrative of Marxist literary criticism. Then, I shall examine the area of Clare and Gramscian theory applied to labouring class poetics, especially, the 'enclosure elegies' but also beyond this subgroup of Clare's poetry where relevant. That of two of his contemporaries, Ann Yearsley, and Robert Bloomfield. Here the relationship between Ann Yearsley and her patron, Hannah Moore, will be pertinent. Therefore, the nature of patronage in labouring class poetics. Also, John Clare and his fraught relationship with John Taylor, notably regarding the question of grammar and dialect, is significant. I will explore Clare's 'madness' in Gramscian terms and, finally, explore the rupture between Marxist theory and the proletariat today, which is a pressing one, I argue. I will examine the prospects for a society where all can achieve their complete humanity, whereby the artificial and moribund division of labour between manual and mental labour will be abolished over time. Thus, this would allow the conditions for the transcending of John Clare's 'double alienation' from both his rustic roots and the literati. Finally, Clare's radical concern for ecology as delineated in To a Fallen Elm is echoed in Charlotte Mew's The Tree are Down . Charlotte Mew's poem like some of Clare's asylum poems is foreshadowing a certain demise. Both poems exhibit an extraordinary and profound discourse between the speaker and the natural world. As far as Mew's epigram is concerned from the Book of Revelation it is of interest that Clare was involved with the Non-Conformist Christian group 'The Ranters' for a period in the late 1820s and early 1830s but not as early as 1820 as claimed by the Tibbles. This turn to a radical Christian sect was adequately informed by E.P. Thompson as 'the chiliasm of despair' in The Making of the English Working Class.

Chapter sequence.

Introduction:
I make a new contribution to the scholarship on John Clare by placing it in a Gramscian context. This methodology cannot be abstracted from the narrative of Marxist literary criticism and philosophy or its concrete conditions. I will illustrate seven main areas.

Chapter One. In search of a method.
I position my argument in the intertextual discourse of Marx & Engels, Plekhanov & Lenin, and Trotsky and Antonio Gramsci. Also, in the Anglophone tradition: Christopher Caudwell, E.P. Thompson, Raymond Williams, Perry Anderson, John Molyneux, and Alex Callinicos.

Chapter Two. The pen and the sword.
I shall delineate John Clare's resistance to 'enclosure' and matters such as Byron's attack on the Labouring Class poets and understand these in Gramscian terms. Also, in this chapter, I shall explore the 'mosaic' (Gramsci) of folklore and its relationship to the role of the subaltern 'counter-hegemonic organic intellectual.' In the former case, as illustrated below in Alberto Mario Cirese (2022) Gramsci's Observations on folklore, Conceptions of the world, spontaneous philosophy, and class instinct . He juxtaposes the folkloric tradition with the hegemonic:
folkloric versus official
(active or passive) versus (active or passive)
subaltern versus hegemonic
simple versus cultured
unorganic versus organic
fragmentary versus unitary
implicit versus explicit
debased versus original.
Whereas the counter-hegemonic organic Intellectual, in the last instance, contests hegemony with the terrain of the ethnopolitical elite.

Chapter Three. 'Money bags.'
The question of patronage was a thorny one affecting Yearsley and Moore. But was generalized to all labouring class poets. Kerri Andrews (2015) Ann Yearsley and Hannah More, Patronage and Poetry Routledge, London, will be seen as a valuable secondary source.

Chapter Four. Grammar or Grammer.
…grammer in learning is like Tyranny in Government.
                              - John Clare.
In this chapter, I will explore John Clare's counter-hegemonic 'voice' regarding his dialect and grammar and his attempts to defend it. The work of James C. McKusick, John Clare, and the Tyranny of Grammar will be understood as a significant resource:
https://www.proquest.com/docview/1297400775?parentSess ionId=IEQIDHCnQfQcGqALrfFV1ZgCW%2Fbyij5SiexVc291 JTw%3D&pq-origsite=primo&accountid=14697

Chapter Five. Madness or double alienation.
Clare's opinion of Northampton County Lunatic Asylum was as follows:

                …there was never a more disgraceful deception than this place. The purgatorial hell & French Bastille of English liberty.

In this chapter, I will examine strands of Clare's 'madness' as an unstable counter-hegemony and also employ Classical Marxism's resources. Sara Lodge suggested that clinically, Clare might have experienced Cyclothymia which would not have justified hospitalization. I will investigate Clare's double alienation from his community and the literati, which will be understood in dialectical terms. Then it will be examined in the light of John Molyneux's (2021) The Dialectics of Art. Here Molyneux developed an innovative contribution to aesthetics with poetry being understood as non-alienated labour under capitalism when unified dialectically with 'Form and Content.' Marx argued that 'Milton wrote Paradise Lost in the manner that a silkworm produces silk. Of its nature.' Therefore, Clare's 'madness' and double alienation may have been misunderstood. Bate (2003 p. 476) maintained that the reminiscences of a fellow patient, James Jerome provided valuable data which challenged the dominant narrative regarding Clare's illness, placing him in a more favourable light.

Chapter Six. Western Marxism: results and prospects., Following: Perry Anderson, (1976) Considerations on Western Marxism.
Alex Callinicos (2021), Routledge Handbook of Marxism and Post-Marxism.
 John Molyneux (2022) Selected Works: Essays on Socialism and Revolution.
I also note the manner of Gramsci's assimilation into some areas of academia:
The conversion of an unrepentant Communist militant…into a harmless gadfly is undoubtedly among the most bizarre and distasteful episodes of recent intellectual fashion.
-          P D Thomas, The Gramscian Moment, London, 2009, p 57fn.
I argue that since the failure of the October Revolution to spread to the advanced Western capitalist areas, there has been a growing gap between Marxist theory and the proletariat in the West.

Chapter Seven. The conditions for John Clare's flourishing and the resolving of his double alienation under Socialism.
It is difficult to predict the extent of self-government which the man of the future may reach or the heights to which he may carry his technique. Social construction and psycho-physical self-education will become two aspects of one and the same process. All the arts – literature, drama, painting, music and architecture will lend this process a beautiful form. More correctly, the shell in which the cultural construction and self-education of Communist man will be enclosed, will develop all the vital elements of contemporary

art to the highest point. Man will become immeasurably stronger, wiser and subtler; his body will become more harmonized, his movements more rhythmic, his voice more musical. The forms of life will become dynamically dramatic. The average human type will rise to the heights of Aristotle, a Goethe or a Marx. And above this ridge, new peaks will rise.

Trotsky (1924)
https://www.marxists.org/archive/trotsky/1924/lit_revo/ch08.htm

Furthermore, Clare's affinity with Nature and his opposition to enclosure provides insight into how, in a socialist society based on need and not accumulation, the impending climate catastrophe could be averted.
My inspiration is derived from E.P. Thompson:
I am seeking to resume the poor, the "obsolete" hand-loom weaver, the "utopian" artisan, and even the deluded follower of Joanna Southcott from the enormous condescension of prosperity.
The general methodology is drawn from Marx's Preface to A Contribution to the Critique of Political Economy (1859):
In the social production of their life, men enter into definite relations that are indispensable and independent of their will, relations of production which correspond to a definite stage of development of their material forces... The mode of production conditions the social, political, and intellectual life process in general.
- Karl Marx .

Therefore, I note Christopher Caudwell, in his early study of Marxian poetics, argued:
There is no neutral world of art, free from categories or determining causes. Art is a social activity... You must choose between class art which is unconscious of its causality and is therefore to that extent false and unfree, and proletarian art, which is becoming conscious of its causality

and will consequently emerge as the truly free art of communism....
However, following the publication of Antonio Gramsci's theoretical material in English, Raymond Williams would suggest, and I agree, that:

>Gramsci's work...is one of the major turning points in Marxist cultural
>history.

Thus, my argument furthers the scholarship on John Clare because it develops a Gramscian strand in that research and into the labouring class poetics more generally.

I shall illustrate that the term hegemony was not employed by Marx or Engels, although they did, of course, construct the argument of the artificial 'division of labour' between manual and mental labour as well as their conceptualization of 'ideology' in The German Ideology The German Ideology - Marxists which Gramsci would not have been able to access. The term came into use with Georgi Plekhanov in the 1880s and then with Lenin. This was the context in which Antonio Gramsci constructed his revolutionary and mould-breaking theory. Gramsci's ideas on intellectuals originated from Lenin (1901/1902). What is to be Done?

>[...] all distinctions between workers and intellectuals... must
>be obliterated.
>-   V.I. Lenin.

See also Chris Harman:

>The greatest modern theoretician of the philosophy of practice [i.e. Lenin] has in opposition to the various tendencies of economism...constructed the doctrine of hegemony as a complement to the theory of the state-as-force.

Although it is clear that for Gramsci, the state, rather than simply being 'a body of armed men' as Lenin had argued, was:

>'the entire complex of practical and theoretical activities with which the ruling class not only justifies and maintains its

dominance but manages to win the active consent of those over whom it rules.' i.e. hegemony.

Gramsci (1971) Selections from Prison Notebooks, p.244).

Although the Prison Notebooks presents two views of hegemony. Thus, the notion of hegemony can usefully be sketched using algebraic terms: Hegemony = consent + coercion = civil society + political society. Gramsci employs the formula: 'State = political society + civil society; in other words, hegemony is protected by the armour of coercion.' Antonio Gramsci delineated his theory of the organic intellectual in the context of his concept of hegemony, as explained here:

The general conclusion is thus clear: for a class to achieve hegemony, it has to create its own organic intellectuals who give that class consciousness of its role and educate it beyond the limited range of what Gramsci calls the 'economic-corporate level.'

As Gramsci poses the primary question about the nature of intellectuals, thus:

Are intellectuals an autonomous and independent social group, or does every social group have its own particular specialized category of intellectuals? The problem is a complex one, because of the variety of forms assumed to date by the real historical process of formation of the different categories of intellectuals.

Although it is important to recognize that Gramsci generally differentiated between the conditions pertaining to the 'East' (Tsarist Russia) about,' (Western Europe) in his epoch, his ideas here have, however, been positioned within two further Gramscian concepts. Firstly, a 'war of movement' and, secondly, a 'war of position.' The former term relates to Tsarist Russia, where the rule was by coercion rather than hegemony and was, thus, prone to a 'frontal assault,' i.e., the Bolshevik Revolution. The latter phrase refers to Western Europe, where a 'war of position' is necessary. Hence the revolutionary struggle became subsumed within a 'siege war' wherein the ideological and cultural struggles would be the necessary counter-hegemonic prerequisites for the coming revolution. Here we see Gramsci understanding the very concept of revolution in the 'West' as a continuum. It is important to emphasize that Gramsci's theorization of the West was not Reformist. He burrowed phrases from World War One and applied them to the class struggle. Later, I will examine the perspectives from (Anderson, 1976) and (Molyneux, 2022), explaining both the nature of Western Marxism and its rupture with proletarian activity. I would note Alex Callinicos's (2021), The Routledge Handbook on Marxism and Post Marxism argues for a new and fifth rendezvous between Marxist theory and the oppressed masses.

Hence, given the theoretical persuasiveness of Gramsci's ideas here. It becomes apparent these ideas are the shining path by which it is possible to illuminate women like Ann Yearsley and men like Robert Bloomfield and John Clare's Labouring Class Romantic poetry as they waged a counter-hegemonic 'war of position' against capitalism. Yearsley, Bloomfield, and Clare were not in what Marx, referring to Shelley, had called 'the revolutionary vanguard.' They had no 'vanguard' organization nor the advantages that poets like Shelley, from the aristocracy, and Keats, the rising bourgeoisie, had bestowed upon them. Also, the proletariat had not, yet, coalesced into the instrument of social transformation. So, these poets were 'counter-hegemonic' in the sense that a 'war of position' was their only option if they were not to be bludgeoned into submission and obscurity in their epoch.

Therefore, I shall argue that John Clare was an 'organic intellectual' who, in the 'enclosure elegies,' his relations with patrons and publishers and in the 'asylum poems' was a counter-hegemonic voice. Here is an example of an enclosure elegy, although, as Sara Guyer (2015, p. 80) notes, 'the Enclosure Act of 1809 was only implemented in 1820, the year in which Clare's first volume of poetry was published.' However, it is central to my account of the first strand within Clare's 'counter-hegemonic account as follows:

Enclosure came, and trampled on the grave /

    Of labour's rights/ left the poor a slave. [...]
 A board sticks up to notice 'no road here.'
 And on the tree with ivy overhung
 The hated sign by vulgar taste is hung
 As though the very birds should learn to know
 When they go there, they must no further go...

The phrase 'enclosure elegies' emanated from Johannes Clare's (1987) John Clare and the Bounds of Circumstance. The nature of his counter-hegemonic struggle can be understood herein in his trespassing poetry. We can see John Clare in The Village Minstrel, (1823) stanza 102, articulating three years after the Enclosure Act was enforced, a nascent proletarian class consciousness:
 The toil-worn thresher, in his little cot
 Whose roof did shield his birth, and still remains
 His dwelling place, how rough soe'er his lot,
His toil though hard, and small the wage he gains
How would he turn and look, and linger there,
 And wish e'en now his cot and poverty to share.
That many a child most piningly maintains;
Send him to distant scenes and better fare,
 How would his bosom yearn with parting-pains
Although this was reminiscent of Wordsworth's (1798), The Ruined Cottage, I would argue. John Taylor, Clare's publisher, as noted in John Clare, The Trespasser (John Goodridge and R.K.R Thornton, 2016, p.59), wrote in the manuscript: 'This is radical Slang.' Therefore, we can observe the class differentiation and the power relationship between the publisher and the published.
 Here I show Byron's assault on Labouring class poets:
 Lo! Burns and, nay, a greater far,
 Gifford was born beneath an adverse star,
Forsook the labours of a servile state,
Stemmed the rude storm, and triumphed over Pate:
Then why no more? if Phoebes smiled on you,
Bloomfield! why not on brother Nathan too?
Him too the Mania, not the Muse, has seized;
Not inspiration, but a mind diseased:

And now no Boor can seek his last abode,
No common be enclosed without an ode.
And in contrast, John Clare wrote about his fellow Labouring
Class poet, Robert Bloomfield. The change in both language
and tone is stark:

Our English Theocritus, Bloomfield.
Thus, I show the class struggle was intense on occasion, for
as Marx and Engels (1848) Communist Manifesto argued:
The history of all hitherto existing society is the history of
class struggles. Freeman and slave, patrician and plebeian,
lord and serf, guild-master, and journeyman, in a word,
oppressor and oppressed, stood in constant opposition to
one another, carried on an uninterrupted, now hidden, now
open fight, a fight that each time ended, either in a
revolutionary reconstitution of society at large or in the
common ruin of the contending classes.

Clare's conflicts with various patrons were reminiscent
of Ann Yearsley and Hannah Moore:
The parallels between Yearsley and Bloomfield...as well as
Clare... suggest Yearsley was not particularly belligerent or
ungracious. Indeed, she might usefully be seen as the most
public face of what appear to have been relatively
commonplace tensions and disagreements which ran
through patronage relationships towards the end of the
eighteenth century.

I also delineate his efforts and contestation with the
publisher, John Taylor, over attempts to preserve his dialect
and original grammar. An example of attempts by Clare to
reject the 'hegemony of Official Standard English' (Tom
Paulin (1992) John Clare in Babylon pp.47-55) is in a letter
to Taylor dated 21st February 1822 in which he wrote:
[misspelling grammar] 'Grammer in learning is like Tyranny
in government' (1951) [eds] Tibble J.W & Anne, The Letters
of John Clare, p.133. In this context, I note: James C.
McKusick, John Clare and the Tyranny of Grammar:
It Is the locality of Clare's dialect that irritates his critics; the
Scottish dialect, having a distinct national character, poses
no threat to England's national identity. But if the "rustics" of
Northamptonshire, Lancashire, and Somerset are allowed to

publish their local dialects, the cultural and linguistic hegemony of London will be exposed and eventually destabilized. These are some of the latent political issues at stake in Taylor's editing of Clare's poetry.

I agree with John Goodridge (2013) John Clare and Community regarding
the dialectics of Labouring Class poetics between classes but also between isolation
and collectivism both between classes and within those classes. I show that Clare's
sense of isolation from his class is illustrated in his prose (note his spelling of 'cumb
for 'come'):

As I did not like to let anybody see me reading on the road of a working day I cumb …into Burghley Park and nestled at the wall side.

John Clare's madness can be perceived as a counter-hegemonic instability. It consisted of two major currents. Firstly, his 'delusion' that his childhood sweetheart Mary Joyce was a 'second wife.' In order to marry her, he absconded from the High Beech private lunatic asylum on 20th July 1841. He might have met a young Tennyson during his stay (Bate, 2005, pp.431-432)
but after leaving walked eighty miles, sometimes living on grass, eating nothing for a forty-eight-hour period, only to find she had died in 1838 in a house fire. In Clare's epoch and circumstances, he could not have known she was dead when he absconded from High Beech asylum, although he thought he had glimpsed her twelve months earlier. I postulate that Byron would not have been detained in an asylum for believing that he had more than one wife. It was a question of class and behaving in a fashion not appropriate to a 'peasant poet.' He was behaving in a counter-hegemonic manner which was an element that led to his detention in Northamptonshire County Lunatic Asylum, where he would stay until his death twenty-three years later. He wrote between eight hundred and one hundred and seventy-six asylum poems while incarcerated privately in

both asylums. Those surviving are contained in Poems of
John Clare's madness, ed. with an introduction by Geoffrey
Grigson (London, 1949) and Poems of the Later Period
(1964) eds Eric Robinson & Geoffrey Summerfield. His
second period of hospitalization was paid for by Lord
Fitzwilliam at eleven shillings a week in Northamptonshire
Lunatic Asylum. The official reason for his detention was
recorded as:
                A farmer addicted to Poetical prossing
The question of multiple personalities arose as Clare was
recorded as saying:
                I am John Clare now. I was Byron and
Shakespeare formerly. At different times you know I am
different people
                – that is the same person with different
names
Clare would describe the latter hospital as follows:
                …there was never a more disgraceful deception
than this place.
                The purgatorial hell & French Bastille of English
liberty.
Therefore, I argue that to utilize Gramsci:
                All men are intellectuals; one could
therefore say: but not all men have in society the function of
intellectuals.
-        Antonio Gramsci

    Retrospectively, Perry Anderson encapsulated the two
distinct traits of Western Marxism, which of course, Gramsci
was a leading theoretical practitioner of as well as an
activist:

The circle of traits defining Western Marxism as a distinct
tradition can now be summarised. Born of the failure of the
proletarian revolution in the advanced zones of European
capitalism after the First World War, it developed an ever-
increasing scission between socialist theory and working-
class practice.

Therefore, I have attempted to construct a Gramscian analysis of John Clare within the narrative of Labouring Class Poetry. As well as an explanation of what John Molyneux (Molyneux, 2022, p.45) has designated as 'the rift between socialism and the working class.' Although it is worth assimilating the data regarding the size of the working class, which is now far larger than when Marx and Engels in the Communist Manifesto argued (Helen Macfarlane's translation, 1851), 'Proletarians of the world unite.' Hence, it is possible to argue that there is the potential for a fifth revolutionary rendezvous between Marxism and the proletariat, as Alex Callinicos (2021) suggested:
The evident conflict between the logic of capital and the urgent necessity of reconstructing our economies to begin to heal the metabolic rift from which spring the catastrophes now cascading on us offers probably the most promising terrain on which Marxist ideas, in no doubt some unanticipated form, can become a material force once again.
 Both my study of John Clare's poetry and of the theoretical apparatus employed, as well as the problems identified within Marxist theory, such as its reception by the proletariat in Western conditions, further the current scholarship, and this, could create a rich theoretical current for other researchers.

Nevertheless, I also argue that The Law of the Tendency of the Rate of Profit to Fall, as discovered by Marx, will create the objective conditions for socialism, but as Trotsky (1938) The Transitional Program noted that it is often subjective factors like, for instance, 'the immaturity of the proletariat.' (Trotsky,1938) that influence the harvesting of ripe objective economic conditions for the creation of international socialism. Nevertheless, a combination of economic crises and dialectical clashes of oppressed and oppressor means the circumstance for socialism will reoccur and either succeed or, quoting Marx: 'lead to the common ruin of the contending classes.'

 In conclusion, I argue that someone like John Clare, although a counter-hegemonic organic intellectual, would only resolve his inner contradictions in a socialist society, as argued by Trotsky (1924). Here he suggested that every person would become 'an Aristotle, a Goethe, a Marx '. It is only then that we can become fully human, I suggest. Nevertheless, I return to the Prison Notebooks of Antonio Gramsci:

In reality, one can only scientifically foresee the struggle but not the concrete moments of the struggle'

Finally, I note that Gramsci complexified the Leninist theory of the State and the relationships of power: For Gramsci, the state, rather than simply being 'a body of armed men' as Lenin had argued, was:

'the entire complex of practical and theoretical activities with which the ruling class not only justifies and maintains its dominance but manages to win the active consent of those over whom it rules.' i.e. hegemony.

((1971) Selections from Prison Notebooks, p.244). These are the limitations of Marxist theory, therefore, of possible human knowledge. This noteworthy poem, written in Northamptonshire County Lunatic Asylum, illustrates the devastation that was inflicted upon Clare for being a counter-hegemonic organic intellectual:

I Am!
I am—yet what I am none cares or knows;
My friends forsake me like a memory lost:
I am the self-consumer of my woes—
They rise and vanish in oblivious host,
Like shadows in love's frenzied stifled throes
And yet I am, and live—like vapours tossed

Into the nothingness of scorn and noise,
Into the living sea of waking dreams,
Where there is neither sense of life or joys,
But the vast shipwreck of my life's esteems;
Even the dearest that I loved the best
Are strange—nay, rather, stranger than the rest. […].

Swimming against the stream is always a challenge especially if, firstly you are not part of a revolutionary wave in what Gramsci called 'an organic crisis' where a new counter-hegemonic 'social block' contests power on the 'ethnopolitical' level and secondary if you, like Clare, are torn by 'contradictory consciousness' as Gramsci explained thus: two theoretical consciousnesses (or one contradictory consciousness): one which is implicit in his activity and which in reality unites him with all his fellow-workers in the practical transformation of the real world; and one, superficially explicit or verbal, which he has inherited from the past and uncritically absorbed. But this verbal conception is not without consequences. It holds together a specific social group, it influences moral conduct and the direction of will, with varying efficacy but often powerful enough to produce a situation in which the contradictory state of consciousness does not permit of any action, any decision or any choice, and produces a condition of moral and political passivity.

Appendix 1.

The research questions and concepts that supply the underpinnings of this doctoral proposal are, firstly, why should I endeavor to construct a reading of John Clare? This was answered in the secondary literature by E. P. Thompson (1968, p.13) The Making of the English Working Class: 'recover from the enormous condescension of prosperity.' Secondly, what is my method and why? I place my response in the intertextual discourse of Marxist Literary criticism. An innovative development within this tradition was mentioned by Raymond Williams (1977), Marxism and Literature: 'Gramsci….is one of the major turning points in Marxist cultural theory.' Thirdly, why does Gramsci's explanatory framework assist in supplying a satisfactory model for enhanced reading of John Clare's contribution to English Literature? This is because he developed the ground-breaking idea of Hegemony and associated it with the innovative concept of the 'counter-hegemonic organic intellectual.' Thus, I question the reading of Joanne Clare's (1987) John Clare and the Bounds of Circumstance, in which she argues that Clare, although aware of his class identity, was not a revolutionary poet. Was Clare a revolutionary poet? Possibly not in the manner that Marx described Shelley as 'being in the revolutionary vanguard.' He did not have the social advantages that Shelley possessed and, rather to utilize Gramsci's terminology, fought a 'war of position' rather than an overt one, a war of movement' as pursued by the aristocracy and nascent bourgeoisie such as John Keats.

Another research question is whether Clare was mentally ill to the point of hospitalization. Sara Lodge argues that he may have experienced Cyclothymia which would not have justified detention in asylums. This is congruent with Clare's letters. So, I argue there is a synthesis between John Clare's life and the contemporary 'lived experience ' of numerous psychiatric patients in modernity.

However, my research questions spread further than the individualization of one member of a social collectivity, labouring class poets of the Romantic Period. My thesis will ask and answer questions such as those of women labouring class poets like Ann Yearsley. Their writing and life. In particular, the question of patronage was relevant to all Labouring Class poets of this period and which, I note, Dickens, in his one reference to John Clare, was scornful. Regarding women poets. What was their attitude to social and gender questions in their epoch? What was the reception of women's Labouring Class Romantic poetry, and did it differ from that of men like John Clare and Robert Bloomfield?

Returning specifically to John Clare, I am interested in his relationship with his editor, John Taylor, especially regarding questions of editing and grammar. This, I shall contend, was an arena for class contestation.

My concluding section of research investigations covers two fields, closely related, to my methodology. Firstly, the nature and failure of Western Marxism to make a connection with the proletariat and, what would be the nature of social formulation which would favour poets, indeed humanity. The question of ecology is a pertinent one.

Appendix 2.

An excellent quote on the 'philosophy of praxis':

… at the level of theory Philosophy of Praxis cannot be confounded with or reduced
to any other philosophy. Its originality lies not only in its transcending
of previous philosophies but also and above all in that it opens up a
completely new road, renewing from head to toe the whole way of
conceiving philosophy itself.
 - Antonio Gramsci.

The philosophy of an epoch… is, therefore, nothing other than the
'history' of that epoch itself, nothing other than the mass of variations
that the leading group has succeeded in imposing on preceding reality.
History and philosophy are in this sense indivisible. They form a 'bloc'.
 - Antonio Gramsc

Appendix 3.

Autumn

The thistledown's flying, though the winds are all still,
On the green grass now lying, now mounting the hill,
The spring from the fountain now boils like a pot;
Through stones past the counting it bubbles red-hot.

The ground parched and cracked is like overbaked bread,
The greensward all wracked is, bents dried up and dead.
The fallow fields glitter like water indeed,
And gossamers twitter, flung from weed unto weed.

Hill-tops like hot iron glitter bright in the sun,
And the rivers we're eying burn to gold as they run;
Burning hot is the ground, liquid gold is the air;
Whoever looks round sees Eternity there.

This belongs to the group of poems written while Clare was confined in the Northampton County Asylum from 1842 until his death in 1864.

Here we can comprehend Clare's transforming 'weeds' i.e., commoners into an integral aspect of their environment. Here Clare overcomes the alienation of man, the subject, and nature, the object with a holistic, indeed, organic understanding. In Gramscian terms, Clare has written beyond the fragmentary and inorganic 'mosaic' of 'folk culture' to provide an innovative reading by a 'counter-hegemonic organic intellectual.' The authentic 'gold' of Nature is seen as elemental in contrast to the gold of the bourgeois literati and that of those in power over him in Northampton
County Asylum.
A Vision.

I lost the love of heaven above,
I spurned the lust of earth below,

I felt the sweets of fancied love
And hell itself my only foe.

I lost earth's joys but felt the glow
Of heaven's flame abound in me
Till loveliness and I did grow
The bard of immortality.

I loved but woman fell away
I hid me from her faded fame,
I snatched the sun's eternal ray
And wrote till earth was but a name

In every language upon earth,
On every shore, o'er every sea,
I give my name immortal birth
And kept my spirit with the free.

In another asylum poem, Clare attempts to create an ordered poetic form for his 'contradictory consciousness' (Gramsci). It is of note that the first three stanzas use anaphora in the repeated 'I's. He is a poet alone, alienated in Feuerbachian terms from 'heaven above' but locates his 'species-being' (Marx) in writing. There is a certain ambiguity about women which can also be found in his two Byronic poems
 Don Juan and Childe Harold's Pilgrimage which were both composed in High Beech private asylum. It is written in iambic tetrameter rhyming abab bcbX cdcd ecec. The anaphoric 'I suggest a possible narcissism but, I would contend, the repeated emphasis on the 'self' suggests a contended 'self' and a 'counter-hegemonic instability.' So, therefore, A Gramscian reading illuminates the reading in both its concept of 'contradictory consciousness' having elements of primitive culture and those of a labouring class poet concluding on line 16: 'And kept my spirit with the free.'

The Lament of Swordy Well.

[...]

Yet worried with a greedy pack
 They rend and delve and tear
The very grass from off my back
    I've scarce a rag to wear....
There was a time my bit of ground
    Made freeman o...e slave...[...]

The gypsies camp was not afraid
    I made his dwelling free
Til vile enclosure came and made
    A parish slave of me...[...]

Clare, in this poem of protest and pain, employs his intimate knowledge of Swordy Well to not merely rebuke the act of enclosing the land and, thus, carving up both the land itself and the tradition of the 'open field system' in which three fields would be rotated by those who worked them. Also, leaving a piece of 'common land' on which the local agricultural workers could hold festivals, herd a cow, or suchlike. This, the enclosing of land so amended by Clare was felt deeply. It was the destruction of the life he and those before him had known. That is not to construct a rustic idyll because living off the land was hard. However, the whole sense of community was swept away by this privatization of the common land and commodification of the open field system. This is precisely why Clare personified Swordy Well. It was an integral part of him and of the bucolic community. Clare here transcends Wordsworth and Keats in that, although empathetic they looked in from the outside rather with Clare it was an act of mutilation of both his body and mind. In this sense, it can be argued that in defending the past he was looking to a future society based on the village commune. This was not the conception that Lenin or Gramsci argued for but a late letter from Marx does suggest the village commune in Russia could provide a model for a socialist society. Therefore, it could be argued by extension that here Clare was performing the role of an intellectual embedded in his developing class, an 'organic intellectual' to employ Gramsci's phrase.

Appendix 4. On Stuart Hall.

Has been reminded of Stuart Hall's important work on popular culture as a site of contestation. Hall relied on several influences, including the culturalism of British Marxist thinkers like Raymond William and E.P. Thompson, the import of Althusser, possibly most importantly Gramsci's thinking on hegemony and organic intellectuals, but also the 'multi-accentuality' of Volosinov in Marxism and the Philosophy of Language. I did not agree with every dot and comma when I studied for my first degree at the Open University in Political and Social Science when it was under the influence of Hall. Still, there is no doubt he brewed up something intellectually potent. In the last instance, much of his thinking can be understood as a product of the British working class in a 'downturn'(Tony Cliff) and the lack of sophisticated Trotskyist analysis. Nevertheless, he is remembered as an important Left thinker.

The 'organic intellectual' must work on two fronts at one and

the same time. On the one hand, he has to be at the forefront

of intellectual, theoretical work...But the second aspect is just

as crucial: that the organic intellectual cannot absolve himself

or herself of transmitting those ideas, that knowledge...to those

who do not belong, professionally, in the intellectual class?
-       Stuart Hall (1992) Cultural studies and its theoretical legacies, p.281.

Stuart Hall on Popular Culture in the context of Gramsci' 'hegemony.'
Because popular culture is 'relational', not static in its orientation to the 'ruling bloc.' It is the most important arena for class contestation. However, there is, therefore, no

binary opposition in manners of understanding popular culture:

a)   The obvious definition of popular culture understands the 'masses' as 'cultural dopes' unable to discern the quality of cultural artefacts thrown at them. Storey (1983) shows that 80% of new album releases fail even with advertising.

b)   The mechanistic Left position proposes that there is an 'authentic proletarian culture' which is 'sighed' with 'resistance that will overthrow the bourgeois culture. This was not Trotsky's position, who believed the proletariat must learn from the bourgeois culture before a proletarian one becomes possible. Bogdanov and the 'Productions' took a different view after October 1917, arguing for a 'proletarian culture.'

c)   For Hall the site of popular culture does not have a fixed inherent nature:

                 popular forms become enhanced (and degraded) in cultural value,
                 go up and down the cultural escalator.
-       Stuart Hall (1981) Notes on deconstructing the popular. p.234

Bibliography.

Primary Sources:

Bloomfield, Robert (1916) Poems: a collection [unknown].
Bloomfield, Robert (1947) A Selection of Poems, London, The Grey Wall Press.
Bloomfield, Robert (2007) Selected Poems, Nottingham, Nottingham Trent University.
Byron. English Bards, and Scotch Reviewers: A Satire. (Kindle Locations 640-644). Printed for James Cawthorn. Kindle Edition.
Clare, John...
1. Poems descriptive of rural life and scenery (London, 1820).
2. The village minstrel and other poems [2v.] (London, 1821).
3. The shepherd's calendar: with village stories and other poems (London, 1827).
4. The rural muse: poems (London, 1835).
5. Life and remains of John Clare: the Northamptonshire peasant poet, by J.L. Cherry (London, 1873).
6. Poems, ed. with an introduction by Arthur Symons (London, 1908).
7. Poems, chiefly from the manuscript, ed. by Edmund Blunden and Alan Porter (London, 1920)
8. Madrigals and chronicles, being newly found poems written by John Clare, ed. with a preface and commentary by Edmund Blunden (London, 1924).
9. Sketches in the life of John Clare, written by himself, now first published, with an introduction, notes, and additions by Edmund Blunden (London, 1931).
10. The poems of John Clare, ed. with an introduction by J.W. Tibble [2v.] (London, 1935).
11. Poems of John Clare's madness, ed. with an introduction by Geoffrey Grigson (London, 1949).
12. The letters of John Clare, ed. by J.W. and A. Tibble (London, 1951).

13. The prose of John Clare, ed. by J.W. and A. Tibble (London, 1951).
14. Selected letters, ed. by Mark Storey (Oxford, 1988).
15. The early poems of John Clare: 1804-1822, general ed. Eric Robinson [2v.] (Oxford, 1989).
16. Poems of the middle period, 1822-1837, general ed. Eric Robinson [4v.] (Oxford, 1996-98).
17. Poems of the middle period, 1822-1837, Volume V, general ed. Eric Robinson (Oxford, 2003).
18. Poems of the Later Period (1964) eds Eric Robinson & Geoffrey Summerfield.
19. Clare, John (2013) [ed] Storey, The Critical Heritage. New York, Routledge.
Mew, Charlotte "The Trees are Down" from Collected Poems and Prose (Manchester, England: Carcanet Press Ltd., 1981). https://www.poetryfoundation.org/poems/51731/the-trees-are-down
 Southey, Robert (1836) The Works and Lives of the Uneducated Poets.
Wordsworth, William (2008) William Wordsworth, The Major Works, Oxford, Oxford University Press.
Yearsley, Ann (1931) Poems On Several Occasions, London, Scholar Select.
Yearsley, Ann (1787) Poems on various subjects by Ann Yearsley...being her second collection. British Museum, Ecco Print.
Yearsley, Ann (2003) Selected Poems, University of Gloucestershire, The Cyder Press.

Secondary Sources:

Althusser, Louis (1971) For Marx, London, Allen Lane
Penguin Press.
Althusser, Louis, Ideological State Apparatus
Louis Althusser Ideology And Ideological State Apparatuses
(Notes ...
Anderson, Perry (1976) Considerations on Western Marxism
Perry Anderson : Considerations On Western Marxism
(1976)
Anderson, Perry (2020) The Antinomies of Antonio Gramsci.
London, Verso.
Andrews, Kerry (2015) Ann Yearsley and Hannah More,
Patronage and Poetry Routledge, London.
Bate, Johnathan (2004) John Clare, London. Picador.
Clare, Johanne (1987) John Clare and the Bounds of
Circumstance, Kingston, McGill Queen's University Press.
Callinicos, Alex, (2021), The Routledge Handbook on
Marxism and Post Marxism, London, Routledge.
Caudwell, Christopher (1946) Illusion and Reality, London,
Lawrence, and Wishart.
Empson, Martin (2022), Socialism or Extinction, London,
Bookmarks.
Gramsci, Antonio (1971) Selections from Prison Notebooks.
London, Lawrence & Wishart.
Gramsci, Antonio (1999) The Antonio Gramsci Reader,
London, Lawrence & Wishart.
Gramsci, Antonio in Alfonso Bordello (2020) Gramsci:
Introduction, Villaggio Publishing Ltd. Kindle Edition., p. 5.
Hall, Stuart (1981) Notes on deconstructing the popular, in
R. Samuel (ed) People's History and Socialist History,
London, Routledge.
Hall, Stuart with A. Bailey (1992) Cultural studies and its
theoretical legacies, in Culture Studies, New York,
Routledge.
Harman, Chris, "Gramsci, the Prison Notebooks and
Philosophy", International
 Socialism 114 (spring 2007).

John Clare in Context (1994) Hugh Haughton (Editor), Adam Phillips (Editor), Geoffrey Summerfield (Editor), Cambridge, Cambridge University Press.
https://www.historicalmaterialism.org/blog/intellectuals
Lenin (1901/1902). What is to be Done?
https://www.marxists.org/archive/lenin/works/1901/witbd
Lodge, S Clare, John Clare 1793-1864, ProQuest, Ann Arbor.
 James C. McKusick, John Clare, and the Tyranny of Grammar
https://www.proquest.com/docview/1297400775?parentSessionId=IEQIDHCnQfQcGqALrfFV1ZgCW%2Fbyij5SiexVc291JTw%3D&pq-origsite=primo&accountid=14697
Landry, Donna (1990) The Muses of Resistance: Labouring Class Women's Poetry in Britain 1739-1796, Cambridge, Cambridge University Press.
Marx, Karl & Engels Frederick (1848) Communist Manifesto Manifesto of the Communist Party - Marxists
Marx Karl (1859) Preface to A Contribution to the Critique of Political Economy):
https://www.marxists.org/archive/marx/works/1859/critique-pol-economy/preface.htm
Marx & Engels The German Ideology The German Ideology - Marxists
Molyneux, John (2021) The Dialectics of Art, London, Haymarket.
Molyneux, John (2022) Selected Works: Essays on Socialism and Revolution. London, Bookmarks.
Paulin, Tom (1992) Minotaur: Poetry and the Nation State, London, Faber & Faber.
Paulin, Tom in Guyer, Sara (2015), Reading with John Clare, Biopoetics, Sovereignty, Romanticism (Lit Z) I, USA, Fordham University Press.
Schwarzmantel, John. (2015) The Routledge Guidebook to Gramsci's Prison Notebooks, Taylor, and Francis. Kindle Edition.
Storey, Mark (1974) The Poetry of John Clare: A Critical Introduction. New York MacMillian.

Thomas, P D (2009, The Gramscian Moment, London, Haymarket.

Thompson, E. P (1968) The Making of the English Working Class, revised. Harmondsworth: Pelican Books.

Trotsky (1924)
https://www.marxists.org/archive/trotsky/1924/lit_revo/ch08.htm

Vardy, Alan (2003) John Clare, Politics and Poetry, New York, Palgrave MacMillian.

Waldron, Mary (1996) Lactila, Milkmaid of Clifton: The Life and Writings of Ann Yearsley, USA, University of Georgia Press.

White, Simon (2016) Robert Bloomfield, Romanticism and the Poetry of Community, London, Routledge.

Williams, Raymond (1977) Marxism and Literature. Oxford, Oxford University Press.

The life and ideas of Emma Goldman.

Emma Goldman was a woman who defied those who would oppress humanity generally and her specific contribution to the rise of revolutionary feminism is today of major significance. Her refusal to submit to the jackboot of any ideology she regarded as tyrannical, whether it was American capitalism or what she regarded as mistakes made by the Russian Marxists around the Kronstadt uprising in 1921, is an inspiration to the downtrodden masses today. But revolutionaries never grow old and as a mature woman of 67 she travelled to Spain in 1936 to help organize the defence of the revolution against the fascists and other agents of international Capital. She was both a theoretician and an activist who wrote some of the most important documents of modern anarchism and also spent time in prison because of her refusal to be silenced. Emma was born into a Jewish family living in Lithuania in 1869. But because of the backlash from the state after the assassination of Tsar Alexander 11 in 1881, there was great political oppression and pogroms against Jews, the family moved to St. Petersburg when Emma was 13. As a consequence of their economic hardship she had to leave school after six months and work in a textiles factory. It was here that Emma was introduced to revolutionary ideas and read a novel by Nikolai Chernyshevsky called: What is to be Done The life and ideas of Emma Goldman. Emma Goldman was a woman who defied those who would oppress humanity generally and her specific contribution to the rise of revolutionary feminism is today of major significance. Her refusal to submit to the jackboot of any ideology she regarded as tyrannical, whether it was American capitalism or what she regarded as mistakes made by the Russian Marxists around the Kronstadt uprising in 1921, is an inspiration to the downtrodden masses today. But revolutionaries never grow old and as a mature woman of 67 she travelled to Spain in 1936 to help organize the defence of the revolution against the fascists and other agents of international Capital. She was both a theoretician and an activist who wrote some of the most important documents of modern anarchism and also spent time in prison because of her refusal to be silenced. Emma was

born into a Jewish family living in Lithuania in 1869. But because of the backlash from the state after the assassination of Tsar Alexander 11 in 1881, there was great political oppression and pogroms against Jews, the family moved to St. Petersburg when Emma was 13. As a consequence of their economic hardship she had to leave school after six months and work in a textiles factory. It was here that Emma was introduced to revolutionary ideas and read a novel by Nikolai Chernyshevsky called: What is to be Done in which the heroine Vera becomes a nihilist and lives in a world where there is not any hierarchy in gender relationships and where all work is done on a co-operative basis. These experiences, both emotional and intellectual, would create within Emma a distrust of state authority and a desire for freedom, they created the foundations on which her anarchist politics and philosophy would later be constructed. In 1931 she encapsulated her beliefs succinctly:
"I want freedom, the right to self-expression, everyone's right to beautiful, radiant things".
-       Emma Goldman.
By the age of 15 Emma was becoming a lively young woman, her father's response was to get her married, she refused and consequently her parents decided to send her to America. Emma soon realized that the U.S.A. was not the land of opportunity for the masses, but a capitalist system based on exploitation. She married a fellow factory worker and gained U.S. citizenship. Would her life be worn down into dust by capitalist oppression and patriarchy domination? At the age of 20 things were rather bleak, but in 1886 something occurred which would again ignite the fire within Emma. The anarchist movement in the U.S. was quite active at this time and during a clash between militant workers and the police in Chicago, the workers were demanding an eight-hour day, someone threw a bomb into a group of police.

Eight anarchists were convicted on very flimsy evidence; the judge even told them they were on trail "because you are anarchists". Four anarchist comrades were hung and became known in working-class history as the Haymarket Martyrs. On the day of the verdict Emma decided to become a revolutionary. Her marriage had not been a success, so Emma now divorced her husband, moved to New York and joined the community of anarchist thinkers and activists. Emma was realizing that:

"It requires less mental energy to condemn than to think".
- Emma Goldman.

She was thinking and contemplating action: Having traced Emma Goldman's early years to the point where she embraced revolutionary anarchism I would now like to examine four areas of her thought: 1) Her commitment to the concept of "propaganda by deed" which had been developed by the anarchist thinker and activist Mikhail Bakunin. 2) Emma's analysis of religion and the failure of Christianity. 3) Goldman and the Bolsheviks. 4) Her ideas on the nature of love. Emma was initially attracted to anarchists of the Bakuninite tendency who were, in the U.S., grouped around Johann Most. She embraced many of Mikhail Bakunin's ideas because he had argued that anarchism was the:

"absolute rejection of every authority including that which sacrifices freedom for the convenience of the state."
-        Mikhail Bakunin.

The position he was arguing for here would not be considered particularly militant in revolutionary circles and formed a basic tenet of anarchist philosophy. However Bakunin's ideas of how to achieve the raising of the consciousness of the oppressed from that of their day to day struggles to that of revolutionary action were radical and are still contested by some anarchists and many Marxists in the anti-capitalist movement today, he argued that:

"we must spread our principles, not with words but with deeds, for this is the most popular, the most potent, and the most irresistible form of propaganda."
- Mikhail Bakunin.

This theory was called "propaganda by deed", it was assumed that a revolutionary act, often of individual violence, would arouse the masses to take place in an insurrection and overthrow the existing order. This was an essential component of Bakunin's political philosophy. He followed this argument to its logical conclusion and perceived the revolutionary's emotions of hostility towards the system as a manifestation of creativity:

"The passion for destruction is a creative passion".

- Mikhail Bakunin.

The reason Bakunin's position is criticized by most Marxist revolutionaries is because it detaches an individual activist from the collective nature of working-class struggle. These comrades argue that revolutionaries should organize themselves in a revolutionary party within the most advanced sections of the working class and when historical necessity creates the circumstances this "vanguard" should intervene in a decisive way. This party of organized activists will, it is argued, play a leading role in guiding the proletariat towards its "world historic task" (Engels) of creating the "dictatorship of the proletariat", which is the rule of the majority. Once created a "workers state" will, as objective conditions allow, "wither away" (Engels) to leave a classless society. Both anarchists and Marxists believe that the creation of a society without class or gender hierarchies is the desirable conclusion of social transformation.

Nevertheless, Emma was, at this time, convinced of the truth of Bakunin's theory of "propaganda by deed". While in New York she met Alexander Berkman, a friend of Johann Most and follower of Bakunin, Emma and Alexander became lovers and would remain life-long friends. This core of three intellectuals was committed to the idea of "propaganda by deed". Goldman and Berkman closely followed a violent strike taking place in 1912 known as the 'Homestead Strike'. The workers had occupied the factory but were expelled by gunmen hired by the owners, several workers died in the struggle. Emma and Alexander were enraged; Goldman gives an account of their feelings (Frick was the manager): "We were stunned. We saw at once that the time for our manifesto had passed. Words had lost their meaning in the face of innocent blood spilled. Intuitively each felt what was surging in the heart of the other. Sasha [Alexander Berkman] broke the silence, Emma remembered.

"Frick is the responsible factor in this crime," he said; "he must be made to stand the consequences." It was the psychological moment for an Attentat (i.e., assassination); the whole country was aroused, everybody was considering Frick the perpetrator of a coldblooded murder. A blow aimed at Frick would re-echo in the poorest hovel, would call the attention of the whole world to the real cause behind the Homestead struggle. It would also strike terror in the enemy's ranks and make them realize that the proletariat of America had its avengers".

-Emma Goldman.

Emma then tried, unsuccessfully, to prostitute herself to raise money to buy a gun, but eventually Berkman carried out an unsuccessful assassination attempt for which he was sent to prison for 22 years, being released on parole after 14 years. Berkman had refused to implicate Emma in the action, and she campaigned for his release. Johann Most, who had been at the heart of the Bakuninite movement in the U.S., suddenly changed his position, condemned Berkman in his newspaper and accused him of creating sympathy for Flick. Emma continued with her political activities but was disillusioned with the Bakuninite tactic of "propaganda by deed". She remained an active agitator and shared platforms with the I.W.W. (International Workers of the World) that were an anarcho-syndicalist organization committed to working class struggle. In 1916 Emma was arrested for her feminist activities, she was distributing radical literature to women workers We can see how Emma's Bakuninite tendencies lead her to make errors in the tactics to be employed by revolutionaries. But her refusal to be gagged by the State, patriarchy or capitalist oppression is something which can be admired today.

Next, I would like to examine Emma Goldman's ideas about Atheism and Christianity. Her ideas were fine tuned 1913-16. She was to a considerable degree influenced by Fredrick

Nietzsche who she described as a "great mind". His proclamation that "God was dead" resounded through the world of all thinking people in the modern period. For Nietzsche the problem was once there is not a Divine "first cause" or Creator God for Nature then everything is in chaos. How can human beings live authentically in these circumstances? A part of his answer was derived from his reading of Schopenhauer and the concepts of "appearance" and "reality". Nietzsche applied these concepts to Greek culture: the Apollonian seen as the intellectualizing, the world of "appearances", and the Dionysian as the wild and stormy dimension which is tuned into real life or "reality", the "will-to-life", the creative. It was this "will-to life" that Nietzsche and Goldman believed was being suppressed by Christianity and religion in general. Emma said:

"The Atheists know that life is not fixed, but fluctuating, even as life itself is".

-       Emma Goldman.

This is her recognition of the life-force, the Dionysian as opposed to Apollonian. That is not to suggest that Goldman was not an intellectual, for she most certainly was, but that she was in touch with the essence of life itself. An illustration of this occurred on an occasion when Emma was dancing and a young comrade took her to one side and said that this was not correct behaviour for an agitator, Emma replied:

"Our cause should not expect me to behave like a nun, the movement should not be turned into a cloister, if it means that, I do not want it".

- Emma Goldman

Of Nietzsche she said: "Nietzsche was not a social theorist, but a poet, a rebel and innovator. His aristocracy was neither of birth or purse; it was of the spirit. In this respect Nietzsche was an anarchist". - Emma Goldman. Her views on political violence underwent a further transformation whilst she was in revolutionary Russia in the early 1920s. Goldman had advocated "propaganda by deed" but had renounced it after the debacle of 1912. However, after that period Emma was still in favour of "defensive" working class violence. In revolutionary Russia, she came to the conclusion that the

Bolsheviks had institutionalized political violence and terrorism. Her analysis was: "Such terrorism begets counter-revolution and in turn becomes counter-revolutionary". - Emma Goldman. However, she wrote to Berkman in 1926 that there was only one choice open to people: either to become a Bolshevik or a Tolstoy an (Tolstoy had theorized the "Holy Peasant" as the basic unit of the agrarian anarchy-pacifist commune). Tolstoy had said: 'There is only one permanent revolution and that is a moral one: the regeneration of the inner man". Emma was once asked about her ideas on "free love", she replied: "Free love? As if

love is anything but free! Love is free; it can dwell in no other atmosphere". - Emma Goldman. She went on to define her "free love": "My love is sex, but it is devotion, care, patience, friendship, it is all." - Emma Goldman.
Emma Goldman was not a Marxist. Yet she stands with other great woman of the revolutionary current against oppression.

Alice Walker, The Color Purple.

Alice Walker argues that her emblematic novel 'The Color Purple:
'…remains for me a theological work'.
- Walker, Preface written for the Tenth Anniversary Edition (1992) ix.
Whilst a socialist feminist critique notes that the 'lived experience' of black women is founded on 'triple jeopardy': 'The triple oppression of black women [on the] axis of race, class and gender, through which their subordination and struggle is lived.' - Kaplan, Keeping the Colour in The Color Purple, in Sea Changes, 1986, p181. This analysis will maintain that there is a profound contradiction between the perspective that Walker argues i.e. that 'captive' (Walker/Celia) can be freed by a spiritual 'realization' and a more radical contention that freedom from the dominant ideology of white patriarchal capitalism can only be achieved by social transformation. The latter position is explained by

159

Angela Davis as part of her critique of the limitations of Black Nationalist writing; 'Where cultural representations do not reach out beyond themselves, there is the danger that they will function as the surrogates for activism and that they will constitute both the beginning and the end of practice'. Angela Davis, "Black Nationalism: The Sixties and the Nineties." Black Popular Culture, ed. Gina Dent (Seattle, Wash: Bay Press, 1992), p 324. So, Walker can be perceived as arguing a kind of passivity. The contribution of Louis Althusser theory of 'Ideological state Apparatus' is useful here as it argues we are 'hailed' or 'named' as 'subjects-in-ideology'. by the ISAs. What are the ramifications of this for 'reading text'? 'The subject, therefore, is a social construct, not a natural one. A biological female can have a masculine subjectivity, she can see her place in the world through patriarchal ideology. Similarly, a black person can have a white subjectivity. Literary Theory and Gender: An anthology (1998). p308 But Cara Kaplan points out, once the question of the 'subject' is raised: 'The gendered subject is more rooted in psychological processes, the ideological subject of Althusser in historical and social ones.' ibid. I recognize that a 'positioning' of Walker (1983) in this context leads us back to what Virginia Woolf argued was a specifically' 'feminine' (see Woolf Times Literary Supplement (1923) orientation. Woolf would develop this concept further in her novel To the Lighthouse: 'She imagined how in the champers of mind and heart of the women [where] tablets bearing sacred inscriptions which if one could spell them out, would teach one everything.' - Woolf To the Lighthouse (1927) p 78-9. But a consequence of Woolf's position is that one of the paradoxes within Alice Walker's philosophy of 'Womanism' occurred because it only offers a form of religion as a solution', which Engels argued is: 'The fantastic reflections in people's minds which constitute their daily life, a reflection in which the terrestrial form assumes the form of supernatural forces.' Engels, Anti During in Marx/Engels on Religion (1976) p128 Rather than socio-historical change Walker offers either mysticism or a form of alienation incarnate in the 'American Dream' i.e. Capitalism has the solution to Black people's economic difficulties. Harpo makes; 'Right straight money.' Walker, (1982) p 66. This is highlighted as Walkers' account of 'Celia's firm 'Folkspants Unlimited' is not impacted upon and in the chronology of the story she does mention the 'Wall Street Crash of 1929 and ensuing world historic crisis of capitalism. A close reading will apply this theoretical model and its consequences for the text and Walkers' perspective'. The Color Purple is a masterpiece which broke the mould by bringing Black American Women's writing into the mainstream. But isn't this part of the problem. Let me quote from Simone de Beauvoir the Second Sex (1953); 'A man would never set out to write a book on the peculiar situation of the human male. But if I wish to define myself I must first of all say: 'I am a woman.' Simone de Beauvoir (1953). Walker claims Sojourner Truth, a remarkable ex-slave, who silenced a hostile meeting by exposing her breasts and shouting 'Ain't I a woman' as a 'spiritual ancestor': 'How happy I was when I realized this…I get power from this name that we share.' Walker (1989), Living by the Word p 97-8. A problem with Walker, following de Beauvoir, is that her 'sisterhood' can only be defined by the 'Other' whether it be a Patriarchal God, Man or ultimately Nature as Celia embraces Pantheism; woman is defined by the 'Other'. Sojourner Truth's statement was a rhetorical device which is also used by Walker in her characterization of Celia throughout the novel to illustrate her growing strength and self-realization from the awful: 'Dear God what is happening to me?' The Color Purple p 3. to the self-assured: Dear Nettie, Well, you know where there's a man, there's trouble.' ibid p 175. Here we see the central 'form of the novel, its written as an 'expository novel' in the form of letters from Celia to 'God' who after her repeated 'rape' by 'Pa'. Celia is the 'focalised character' whom the novel revolves. The first line of the novel: You better not never tell nobody but God. It'd kill your mammy ibid 3. Celia's reply takes the form of a letter; 'Dear God, I am fourteen years old. I am… '. ibid. In this Walker 'contextualizes what become this series of letters. Celia response, alone and

frightened, can only be that of the alienated individual crying to God for assistance and the 'woman' being 'interpellated' by the 'Other'. She is obliterated by Patriarchal oppression and the novel will unfold until Celia finally after her two 'realizations: 1) as a woman and 2) as a pantheist which are both facilitated by Shug and Celia can say:
'Amen.' (So be it). ibid 261 Hence Walker is consistent in her use of 'theological' idiom.
The 'point of view employed by Walker is therefore appropriately a 'first person narrator' technique. Celia is the central 'narrator', but her sister Nettle is sometimes, and this provides an atmosphere of intimacy congruent with Walker's concept of 'Womanism'. Hence the 'reader 'has a sympathetic, almost empathetic, relationship to the protagonist Celia and her sister Nettle who is the' minor character'. This 'first person narration' method aspires to creating a sense of 'authenticity' which Walker achieves in Celia. Celia refers to herself in the 'first-person singular. It is important that Walker, the author, should not be regarded as the 'narrator', a technique used by Walker to articulate her concept of 'Womanism''
'Us sleep like sister me and Shug.' ibid p 131. Employing the alliterative repeating of's' sounds which is onomatopoetic, it sounds like 'Sisterhood' with a warm and full resonance. but there is also an element of phonoaesthetic i.e. relating sound and meaning by association. Here the monosyllable us' followed by 'Shug' are related: '.   Hugging is good. Snuggle. All of its good.' ibid. Here Walker employs assonance with the '[H]u' and '[Sn] u again creating a domed rather than 'phallic' sound representative of Celia first 'realization of the 'Divine not being distinct' (Walker Preface) through Shug; lesbianism. Celia's second and concomitant 'realization' of the 'Divine being separate' also is derived from Shug who is a symbol of 'independent womanhood'. Walker uses a short and piece of 'dialogue' as a prelude to this 'epiphany', almost like: 'The Dark Night of the Soul' described so eloquently by St John of the Cross (1968). 'Dear Nettie, I don't write to god no more... what happened to god? ast Shug. Who that? I say ... She talk and talk and

try to bulge me from blasphemy. but I blaspheme as much as I want to.' ' ibid p174. But Shug enlightens her as this animated dialogue, a discourse of black women discovering Divinity in their Image. '... one things in the white folks bible. Shug! I say God wrote the Bible it had nothing to do with white folks ... When I found out god was a man and white I lost interest.' ibid p 175. Shug continues: Yeah, It, god ain't a he or She it's an It. ibid p 176. Then Shug provides the revelation:

'It pisses God off if you walk past by the color purple and don't notice it.' ibid p 177. Hence the 'double realization' achieves fruition; 'sisterhood' and Pantheism'. Walker has used a genre similar to 'melodrama' with a reliance on Jungian 'synchronicity' to articulate her ideology of 'Womanism' and it broke the mould. Elaine Showalter uses a term: 'geocentricism' to describe a framework of 'women's production, motivation and analysis '

Finally, I would agree with Eagleton that: For Marx, 'then, the ability of art to manifest human power is dependent on the moment of History itself.' Eagleton, (1976) p68. The epoch The Color Purple was written in meant it could not act as a catalyst for revolution but was appropriated by the 'Ideological State Apparatus'. Althusser: 'The mirror structure of ideology ensues: 1. The absolute guarantee that everything is real is as so... everything will be alright: Amen 'So be it.' Literary Theory: an anthology (1998) p 302.

Bibliography
Davis, A (1992) Black Nationalism: The Sixties and The Nineties in Black popular Culture, ed Gina Dent, Bay Press.
de Beauvoir, S (1953) 'Introduction', The Second Sex, Pan Books.
Eagleton, T (1976) Marxism and Literary Criticism, Routledge.
Engels, F (1878) Anti-During in' Marx and Engels: On Religion', Progress Publications, Moscow.
Kaplan, C (1986) Keeping the Colour in The Color Purple in, Sea Changes: Essays on Culture and Feminism, Verso.

John of the Cross (1968) The poems of St. John of the Cross, New Directions Paperbook.
Rivkin, J and Ryan, M (eds) (1998) Literary Theory: an anthology, Blackwell.
Walker, A (1998) Living by the Word, Mariner Books.
. Walker, A (1983) The Color Purple, The Woman's Press.
Walker, A (1993) Preface written for the Tenth Anniversary, The Woman's Press.
Woolf, V (1923) Times Literary Supplement. Woolf, V (1927) To the Lighthouse, Vintage.

On Byron Childe Harold's Pilgrimage Canto IV and John Keats' 'Ode to a Grecian Urn'.

'Two souls, alas! are lodged within my breast, which struggle there for undivided reign: One to the world, with obstinate desire, Above the mist the other doth aspire, with sacred vehemence, to purer spheres'. Goethe (1999) Faust 1 ii 40-43.

My analysis will argue that the dialectic delineated by Goethe in 1776-7 which is contained within the individual can be understood as a commentary on Romanticism and can be seen as central to the themes of 'loss and the past' manifest in British Hellenism. This thesis will then be applied to Byron and Keats by 'close reading'. 'This doubleness – poetry-in-itself v. poetry – for – itself and beyond – it - self – is written into Romantic aspiration.' Chandler and McLane (2008) p 7. Sartre concept of 'being – in – itself v being – for – itself' (see Warnock 1965 p 61-2) i.e. 'being –in—itself' has a 'essence', it is real in itself while 'being – for –itself' only exists as far as it goes beyond it-self into 'nothingness'. These concepts are usefully employed here to illustrate the dualism between 'world' and 'pure spheres' and indeed to the nature of the two poems. Byron's Childe Harold's Pilgrimage is understood as existing 'in-itself', the Byronic is anti – Hero is condemned to wander 'in-itself'. Byron is here commenting on Don Juan but it is true of the 'Byronic Hero' generally: 'Almost all is real life, either my own or people I know.' Wu (1998) p 664. While Keats Ode to a Grecian Urn'

is 'for-itself' it transcends it-self into a 'nothingness because as Keats explains in his theory of 'negative capability': 'It is not itself- it has no self – it has everything and nothing.' Owen and Johnston (1998) p 1042. 'It has as much delight in conceiving an Iago as an Imogen.' ibid and therefore in: Ode to a Grecian Urn: 'Beauty is truth, truth beauty…' I 49. ibid. p 396. It is 'beyond - itself'. These poems, therefore, represent a tension between 'essence' and 'existence', Hence they inherently comment on the theme of lose and the past which is rooted in these questions. A fascination with the Greek in relation to the past and present as well as the nature of the imagination was central to the 'second generation' of British Romantic poets:
'The common interest to all varieties of Romantic Hellenism

was an interest in Greece or the Grecian model and a desire to appropriate it to present purpose… this interest was sometimes negative, and sometimes positive, sometimes as a nostalgic yearning, sometimes radical, sometimes conservative.' Ward (1993) p 150.
I shall now examine the relationship of poetic form to the 'past' and 'loss' in the context of my argument in relation to Byron 'Childe Harold's Pilgrimage'. In its title the word 'Childe' is a reference to medieval knights' of noble birth. and suggests a sense of continuity with the past. The selection of Spenserian stanzas alludes to Spencer: 'Fairy Queen' and is subtitled 'A Romaunt'. Both have a resonance with an 'idealized' past, but immediately the poem turns to contemporary themes. The poem exists in-itself, it is itself and nothing else. The body of the work Cantos IV Stanzas 139-144 will now be analysed by a 'close reading'. The general structure of Canto IV is Spenserian stanza rhyming: ABABBCBCC with eight iambic pentameters allthough these can be irregular followed by a longer alexandrine line The Canto IV announces, almost declaims: u / u / u / u / u / 'And here the buzz of eager nations ran,' IV 139: 1143. Owens and Johnson. (1998). p 249 This scans as an iambic pentameter. The rhythm and choice of the verbs 'buzz' and 'eager' to describe the noun 'nations' is declamatory. We are

immediately told that the question of 'nations' will be addressed. In the next line the effect of the use of a Caesura in this sentence makes it apparent that this is not going to be poem applauding the status quo of his day. We will see how this develops into a narrative of the Might and the fall of Rome; itself a biblical narrative of impending catastrophe 'In murmured pity, or loud-roared applause,' IV: 139. 1144 ibid That it is a poem of unresolved dialectical contradictions but is 'for itself' i.e. it is what it is. The line is enhanced by the use in the first half of assonance: with the sounds: 'ur', 'ur' 'e'. These are quite sounding, as is appropriate for pity. The second half in contrast is onomatopoeic; it is the sound of reactionary Nationalism which Byron detested. He then universalizes this theme with a clever combination: 'What matters where we fall to fill the maws IV: 1250. Of worms - on battle-plains or listed sport?' IV: 1251. Several components of these lines are useful to our understanding both of meaning and the devices used to achieve them. The narrator is asking a fundamental question: 'What does it matters when and where and how we die?' How does Byron employ poetic devices to achieve this? The pace of the line 1250 speeds up with the last three iambic feet enhanced by the enjambment into 'of worms' i.e. death line 1251. The reader feels an immediacy of mortality. With 'maws' suggesting 'devouring' or 'greedy' the reader understands that the narrator is speaking of the end rather than any form of transcendence, it is 'poetry – in - itself.' Here we can perceive a complex interweaving of fundamental themes of loss and the past and the nature of the poetic imagination. The reader is now taken on a journey through the rise and fall of Rome: 'A ruin, yet what a ruin! IV: 1279. The repetition of the word 'ruin' combined with an exclamation mark creates a powerful sound to accompany a potent idea. 'The Roman model was again a two-edged sword: splendid and glorious but condemned to fall...Rome was then juxtaposition...of the pure with the savage.' Groom (2008). p 49. This juxtaposition is present in Childe Harold's Pilgrimage as 'life or death', 'revolution or reaction' and with loss and the past. the poem does transcend it-self, it is 'for-itself'.

On Allen Ginsberg, 'Howl' and Trotsky. My argument is stated succinctly and argued to its conclusion. I contest that Allen Ginsberg's Howl was, as some critics argue a popular, 'an over-simplification' of the poetry regarded by the Canon as high-quality literature. Rather, Howl formed a new genre which mirrored in its innovation other seminal moments in literature connected to changes of the 'mode of production' and had similar ramifications. The 'primitive accumulation of capital of English capitalism' that Caudwell (1937) Illusion and Reality associated with William Shakespeare, the 'bourgeois' revolutions that permeate the ideas of Wordsworth (1802) Preface to Lyrical Ballads and the shocks of Darwinism, Freud and imperialist war which informed Modernist literature, particularly the avant-garde pertinently T.S.Eliot (1922) The Waste Land. What was the problem of the writer in late-capitalism as High Modernism entered its death throes? Trotsky (1981) Art and Politics encapsulate it: "The decline of bourgeois society means an intolerable exacerbation of social contradictions, which are transformed inevitably into personal contradictions, art suffers most from the decline and decay of bourgeois society. Art cannot save itself...But precisely in this path history has set a formidable snare for the artist." - Trotsky (1981). p 105. Ginsberg's reply is Howl, this is not the howl of the deranged madman outside of History, it resonates within the conversation of literature, King Lear (1603): "Howl, howl, howl! O, you are men of stones; Had I your tongues and eyes, I'd use them so That heaven's vault should crack." - Shakespeare (1603) (5.3.2.58-64). Howl For Carl Solomon 1 I saw the best minds of my generation destroyed by madness, starving hysterical naked, dragging themselves through the negro streets at dawn looking for an angry fix, angelheaded hipster burning for the ancient heavenly connection to the starry dynamo in the machineery of night - Ginsberg (1956) p. 9 It is the howl of a post-WW 11 avant-garde that must inherently employ the poetic devices of literary tradition but in a different 'form'. A 'close reading' gives us several insights here. They are 'howls' of emotion, of intense emotion and resonate with William Wordsworth (1802) Preface to Lyrical Ballads: "Poetry is the spontaneous overflow of powerful feelings: it takes its origin from emotion recollected in tranquility." - William Wordsworth (1980) pp. 410-424. In Shakespeare (1603) we have a reference to the howling of a man driven to madness seeking justice from 'heaven's vaults'. Ginsberg also seeks refuge in chants to the 'Holy' in Footnote to Howl. The thematic howl of a literate madness, seeking divine justice, but not locating it in a corrupted 'world' runs counterintuitive against the whole Enlightenment project. Surely Reason and empiricist science will hear the poet's words. For Americans like Ginsberg the world could not be explained in these neat confines and as a poet who had read widely he certainly could not accept the text by text alone reductionism of the New Criticism after Hiroshima and McCarthyism, Auschwitz and Stalinism. But what differentiated Ginsberg from other 'Beat' writers in particular Kerouac was that he rejected Kerouac insistence on 'first thought, best thought'. Ginsberg was influenced by both Kerouac in terms of first impulse, but also poets like Eliot, indeed Howl' is an attempt at reproducing something of the literary magnitude of Eliot (1922) The Waste Land. I shall therefore argue against the perspective taken by advocates of Mass Culture Thesis such as the renegade ex-Trotskyist Dwight Macdonald, who argues in (1953) A Theory of Mass Culture and again (1962) Against the American Grain that the collective taste of the 'masses' was reflected in the degraded mass culture that they consumed and that, therefore, they had no 'interest' in 'High Culture'. Dwight Macdonald combined an ex-Trotskyist stance with cultural conservatism and elitism. Also, I argue against a rightist conservative position which is derived from Matthew Arnold (1869) Culture and Anarchy that has an inherent trepidation at the sound of the popular and its revolutionary proclivities. He maintained a 'secular religion' of "The best that has been thought and said in the world." - Arnold (1869) p 6. Was needed to prevent the erosion of civilization. It is no accident that Arnold began his opus magnum in 1867 after a period of popular and vigorous discontent over suffrage rights. Ginsberg's reply here is the 20th century equivalent to an articulate and insurrectionary mob assailing Arnold: "who dreamt and made incarnate gaps in Time & Space through images juxtaposed, and trapped the archangel of the soul between 2 visual images and joined the elemental verbs and set the noun and dash of consciousness together jumping with sensation of Pater Omnipotens Aeterna Deus to recreate the syntax and measure of poor human prose..." - Ginsberg 1956 p 20. Arnold and his Leavisite descendants would be battered and lost for words, their Weltanschauung challenged. Also here we can perceive Ginsberg's specialist use of 'strophes' which he defines as 'a one speech breath thought' which was akin to the jazz improvisation of Miles Davis or Charlie Parker, the black man's 'beat'. 'Form' with a regard for socio-cultural factors would be engaged by the New Historicism of Raymond Williams with his 1958 Forward to Culture and Society: We live in an expanding culture, yet we spend much of our energy regretting the fact, rather than seeking to understand its nature and conditions. - Lodge (1972) p. 580. However, my position is not simply that Mass Culture Thesis and the New Criticism were erroneous, but they failed to understand the nuanced nature of 'proletarian literature' which as Trotsky illustrates is complexified: "Having broken up human relations into atoms, bourgeois society, had a great aim for itself. Personal emancipation was its name. In reality, all modern literature has been nothing but an enlargement of this theme." - Trotsky (1981) pp. 61-62. My position is that only the proletariat has the creative potential and socially universal nature which allowed Marx to say 'communism has solved the riddle of history' can transcend the limitations of the bourgeois intelligentsia when the social and economic conditions are ripe, that is, in a Socialist society because as Marx argued they are the 'universal class'. For the first time in history was there a social collectivity in whose interest it was to dismantle class society, because 'class' fetters on the workers of the world are their 'chains and it is in there interest 'collectively' to break those chains freeing the whole of society. Some Marxists misunderstood the nature of the relationship between the popular and the high cultures. Adorno and Horkheimer in Dialectic of Enlightenment saw an implied analogy between Marx's concept of his fetishized 'exchange value' as a commodity and 'use-value' a 'material object'. Then they extrapolated this analogy to the relationship between popular and high culture to the detriment of the popular. Walter Benjamin is better here, seeing the potential for mechanized reproduction to free the poet from the 'aura' from his or her primitivism and allow an engaged mass readership. Also, I will draw a parallel with Maxim Gorky, Lower Depths (see Raskin 2004 p.82) and Ginsberg Howl, thus Trotsky: "At the beginning, Gorky was imbued with the romantic individualism of the tramp. Nevertheless, he fed the early spring revolutionism of the proletariat on the eve of 1905, because he helped to awaken individuality in that class in which individuality, once awakened, seeks contact with other awakened individualities" - Trotsky (1981) p 58-59 For Trotsky the solution to the dichotomy of oversimplification and complexity in literature is resolved in the synthesis of revolution. Ginsberg, unlike Gorky would not be involved in a social revolution (as he may have wished) but a cultural revolution, a revolution of superstructure rather that of social base which left American capitalism weakened but intact. Louis Althusser (2006) Lenin on Philosophy and Other Essays commenting on the novels of Solzhenitsyn in (Althusser pp.153-153, 2006) makes the point of the difference between art and knowledge. Literature like Solzhenitsyn's, he argues, may have helped the reader 'feel' , 'perceive' the 'cult of personality' in the Soviet Union but doesn't provide the scientific knowledge to understand it. Althusser said art: "In the language of Spinoza it puts the conclusions before the premises." - Althusser (2010) p 153. Ginsberg achieves this by employing and developing poetic devices, Walt Whitman's 'long-line' which is a non-metrical line of poetry of length which usually employs enjambment, anaphora which is a 'figure of repetition' in which the same word is repeated as in Part 1 'Who' usually at the beginning successive 'lines, clauses or sentences' , cauda or the tail-rhyme stanza and a surrealist juxtaposition of images such as 'helium jukebox' (1956).Also Ginsberg aspired to create: 'Certain combinations of words and rhythms actually have "an electrochemical reaction on the body, which could catalyze specific states of consciousness." - Ginsberg (2001) p.31 Brain Jackson (2010) argues: 'the most compelling example of reading "Howl" -specially out loud – is the sene of time shifting from the prosaic to the mythical. Lines such as: "who walked all night with their shoes full of blood on the snowdeck docks waiting for a door in the East River to open to a room full of steamheat opium," - Ginsberg (1956) p. 15 He continues: 'the rhythmic and trouping artifice of Howl constitute...a suspension of time in which the natural laws occur'. - Jackson (2010) pp 312-313). Therefore I maintain that Ginsberg poetry contradicted the ideas of thinkers such as Mathew Arnold, T. S. Eliot, and William Empson's Seven Types of Ambiguity on the Right and renegade Trotskyists like Dwight MacDonald and neo-Marxists Adorno and Horkheimer. I suggest that the neo-Marxism of Louis Althusser enhanced my general understanding of the positioning of the debates regarding the poetry of Ginsberg, particularly Howl and that in this context it is possible to comprehend him in a lineage of literati, Finally I argue that Ginsberg created not a simplified poetry for mass consumption and 'narcotization' of literary consciousness, but formed the matrix for a new genre of second wave of 20th century avant-garde writers who took and added to the High Modernism of 1910-39 and created a wedge into the monotonous conformity of 1950's poetry. Even poets like Sylvia Plath and Anne Sexton who were writing confessional verse which was challenging some conventions in terms of gender and 'content' i.e. mental illness Plath ([1963] 2004) Ariel and Sexton's (1960) 'To Bedlam and part way back' were not really contesting the terrain of bourgeois hegemony. Ginsberg did shift the aesthetics of the hegemonic superstructure cultural construct in favour of the 'progressive', he unlocks much in this poem, but he was unable to create a social revolution. I conclude that the task can only be brought to fruition by the self-emancipation of the proletariat as Leon Trotsky argues in Literature and Revolution: "Under Socialism, Literature and art will be tuned to a different key such as disinterested friendship, this will be the mighty ringing chords of Socialist poetry. However, does not an excess of solidarity, as the Nietzscheans fear, threaten to degenerate man into a sentimental, passive, herd animal? No, not at all. The powerful force of competition this, in bourgeois society, has the character of market competition, will not disappear in a Socialist society, but, to use the language of psycho-analysis, will be sublimated, Art then will become the most perfect ethos for progressive life-building of life in every field." - Leon Trotsky (1981). p 60 The Beats could not vanquish 'Moloch' (essentially, 'Capitalism') but they did undermine, disrupted what Lyotard calls it 'meta-narrative' creating the conditions for minority narratives. Nevertheless, only socialist transformation as understood in the aesthetic writings of Trotsky can create authentic liberation for all of humanity. We may read Ginsberg as a disappointed, reincarnated Maxim Gorky lapsing into a hope for Nirvana with a juxtaposition of the social and questioning 'Who' of Part 1, with the devastation of Moloch only relieved with the introspection of fifteen iambs in two sentences, one 'long-line' without punctuation except the repeated and insistent exclamation marks after each Holy! Footnote to Howl pp 27-8. Ginsberg did provide hope in a new 'beatification' of language within Historical Materialism's philosophy, a new Communist International to resurrect Trotsky's Fourth International... 'holy the Fifth International!' (ibid).

Bibliography. Adorno, T and Horkheimer, M. ([1944] 1979) Dialectic of Enlightenment, trans. by Cumming, London: New Left Books.

Althusser, L (2006) Lenin and Philosophy and other essays, Dahl: Aakar Books. Arnold, M ([1869] 1993) Culture and Anarchy and Other Writings, ed. by S.Collini, Cambridge: Cambridge University Press.

Caudwell, C ([1937]1977) Illusion and Reality, London: Lawrence & Wishart.

Eliot, T.S. ([1920] 1960) The Sacred Wood, London: Macmillan.

Empson, W ([1936] 1966) Seven types of Ambiguity, New York: New Directions. Ginsberg, A ([1956] 2002) Howl and Other Poems, San Francisco: City Lights. Ginsberg, A (2001) Spontaneous Mind: Selected Interviews 1958-1996. New York: HarperCollins. Jackson, A, Modernist Looking: Surreal Impressions in the Poetry of Allen Ginsberg Texas Studies in Literature and Language, Vol. 52, No. 3, Fall 2010. Lodge, J (1972) 20th Century Literary Criticism: A Reader, London: Longman. Lyotard, J.F. (1984) The Postmodern Condition: A Report on Knowledge, trans, by G. Bennington and B. Massumi, Manchester, Manchester University Press.

MacDonald, D (1953) A Theory of Mass Culture, Rosenberg, R. and White D.W (1957) (eds), Mass Culture: The popular arts in America, New York: MacMillan.

MacDonald, D (1962) Against the American Grain, New York: A Da Capo Paperback.

Plath, Sylvia (2004) Ariel: The Restored Edition, London: Faber and Faber.

Ruskin, J (2004) American Scream: Allen Ginsberg's Howl and the making of the Beat Generation, Berkley, University of California Press.

Sexton, A (1960) To Bedlam and part way back, Boston: Houghton Mifflin Company. Shakespeare, William (1603) King Lear. P.

Trotsky, L (1981) On Literature and Art, New York Pathfinder Press.

Wordsworth W (1980) Selected Poetry and Prose of William Wordsworth, New York: Meriden Books